LEARN

BI 3237303 1   X

...ieving QTS

...n Primary Schools

uk

Achieving QTS

Teaching Arts in Primary Schools

Stephanie Penny
Raywen Ford
Lawry Price
Susan Young

First published in 2002 by Learning Matters Ltd.

British Library Cataloguing in Publication Data
A CIP record for this book is available from the British Library.

ISBN 1 903300 35 5

Cover design by Topics – The Creative Partnership
Text design by Code 5 Design Associates
Project management by Deer Park Productions
Typeset by PDQ Typesetting, Newcastle under Lyme
Printed and bound in Great Britain by Bell & Bain Ltd, Glasgow

Learning Matters Ltd
58 Wonford Road
Exeter EX2 4LQ
Tel: 01392 215560
Email: info@learningmatters.co.uk
www.learningmatters.co.uk

CONTENTS

Why teach the arts in primary schools?

Rather than answering this question by defending the place of the arts in the primary curriculum, let us look at a fraction of what we would lose if the arts had no place there.

Without PE, the physical exercise of children would be limited to playground and out-of-school activities. The health and fitness of future generations rely on PE being taught. PE teaches fair play, sharing, the pleasure of participation, the sense of community as well as developing a mastery of skills not achievable by working alone.

Without music, many children would not have the opportunity to participate in muscial activities with others, to develop their skills of playing and singing, to explore their own ways of making music and of coming to know and understand a wide range of music made by others.

Without design and technology, we would lose the ability to invent and create things to solve problems in an effective and holistic way. Science becomes more abstract and meaningless.

Without art and design, we lose the freedom to express our innermost thoughts and fears. Children's knowledge and understanding of artistic and historical movements would be limited to the gamut to which their home life exposes them.

In essence, without the arts we would lose the fabric of creativity, expression of the self and ultimately civilisation. Many would have you believe that they are not academic subjects – that they are easy time-fillers and really only suitable for the 'less able'. In some schools this is believed to the extent that the arts happen only in the odd afternoon; at the end of the calendar year; to occupy those who have finished early; or keep the class happy whilst key players practise the school play. Happily these sorts of school are in the minority. The advent of the National Curriculum ensures a place for the arts under the auspices of the foundation subjects. If we are not to do a disservice to our children then we need to educate and develop the whole child.

How to use this book

This book does not aim to teach you all you need to know about teaching the arts in the primary school: it is a stepping stone, an initiator, a guide.

Each of the core chapters in this book deals with a specific arts subject. Each chapter starts with the rationale given by the Qualifications and Curriculum Authority

(QCA) for that subject's inclusion in the National Curriculum for England. Each chapter then goes on to explore the application of professional values and practice, knowledge and understanding, and teaching skills, to that subject. Close reference is made to the Professional Standards for QTS (TTA/DfES, 2002) that are necessary for the award of Qualified Teacher Status (QTS). For each chapter you will need to have to hand the *National Curriculum Handbook for Primary Teachers* (available at www.nc.uk.net).

Each chapter contains a number of practical tasks. These are designed to encourage you to develop and consolidate your understanding of important skills or issues, and to think carefully about translating some of the theory that you have read into your practice. Some chapters also contain classroom stories that illustrate aspects of the content of the chapter in a classroom context. You will find these useful when considering your own teaching methods and approaches. At the end of each chapter you will find suggestions for further reading, which will enable you to explore particular issues further.

Some aspects of what is required to become a primary teacher are applicable to all of the arts. To avoid needless repetition, these aspects are included in Chapter I. At the end of Chapter I there is an itemised breakdown showing how the Professional Standards relate to the arts.

Chapter 6 gives you the opportunity to audit your professional values, subject knowledge and teaching skills in each arts subject. It is intended to help you identify your strengths and needs in relation to the Professional Standards for QTS and give you some indication of the areas on which you need to focus. Having completed the self-audit you should identify areas for improvement and set specific targets and a time frame in which to achieve them. You may wish to discuss any issues it raises with your mentor.

We hope that you enjoy this book and get a new self-assurance in being able to deliver a most important dimension of our schools' curriculum.

Common requirements

This chapter includes information common to teaching all arts subjects in primary schools in terms of a teacher's responsibilities, planning, teaching and assessment strategies and the requirements all trainees need to achieve to be awarded Qualified Teacher Status.

Aware of and work within statutory frameworks relating to teachers' responsibilities

HEALTH AND SAFETY

The Health and Safety at Work Act, 1974, describes the responsibilities of employers to people who work for them. Within these responsibilities, there is a duty to ensure that:

> '... persons not in ... employment who may be affected are not exposed to risks to their health or safety.'

In other words it is the school that has the responsibility not to expose its pupils to any unacceptable risks regarding personal health and safety.

There are various safety codes in existence for practical activities based mostly on good practice. Teachers have to be aware of dangers and risks, and need to take steps to deal with them. This idea is part of the 'parental' responsibility role that teachers have. The National Curriculum requirements for health and safety states that schools and teachers have to make sure that:

- surfaces, equipment and buildings are safe;
- procedures for safety, first aid and emergencies are in place;
- they are able to explain the steps they take to control risks;
- the activity follows approved and appropriate guidelines and that they take all necessary safety measures;
- parental consent is obtained for trips, outdoor and adventurous activities;
- children are warned of the risks and discouraged from inappropriate behaviour;
- children are prepared properly for the activity. For example, when working with tools, equipment and materials, in practical activities and in different environments, this includes them:
  - knowing about hazards, risks and risk control;
  - being able to recognise hazards, assess consequent risks and take steps to control the risks to themselves and others;
  - being able to use information to assess the immediate and cumulative risks;
  - being able to manage their environment to ensure the health and safety of themselves and others.

Teachers need to know about anything that might affect children taking part in physical activities, including personal fears, asthma, disabilities, diabetes, heart problems, epilepsy, and they need to treat that information confidentially and with understanding of the potential embarrassment for the person involved.

First aid boxes should be available, properly equipped with contents that are regularly checked to maintain provision levels. Teachers are also encouraged to know first aid procedures, and to have a first aid qualification.

Safety requirements for specific activities are available from National Governing Bodies and associations. Some activities, including outdoor pursuits and swimming, require a specific qualification to be held by the teacher, in addition to a recognised teaching certificate or degree.

This also applies to some machines used for cutting and shaping materials. Whilst these are generally not provided in the primary environment, they may be resident in buildings, particularly those that have converted from middle schools.

Social, moral, spiritual and cultural education (SMSC)

Before looking at the role of SMSC in the individual subject areas, it is useful to define the terms.

- *Spiritual development* is concerned with the promotion of opportunities for children to reflect on their lives and the human condition, i.e. what it is that makes us human. It is not confined to the development of religious beliefs, but is about identity and our responses to challenging experiences such as death and suffering through the promotion of wonder.
- *Moral development* relates to children's understanding of the difference between right and wrong, to respect other people, truth, justice and property, and how their understanding is displayed through behaviour and the views they express.
- *Social development* is concerned with the child's growing capacity to relate to others in different social settings in terms of taking responsibility, exercising initiative and working cooperatively and successfully in groups within the school community. Children also need to be made aware of different social structures, such as the family, the school, and local and wider communities.
- *Cultural development* relates to the child's perceptions of cultural environments, and the manifestation of religious, social, aesthetic or ethnic understandings through art, literature, music, dance and other forms.

Citizenship

The 1988 Education Act asserted that children should experience a broad and balanced curriculum that 'prepares ... pupils for the opportunities, responsibilities and experiences of adult life, clearly paving the way for education for citizenship'. The 'opportunities, responsibilities and experiences of adult life' are enormously varied, but clearly the statement calls for education beyond subjects to the education of the whole person in a way that enables them to make a positive and valuable contribution to society. The kinds of experiences that might come within this notion are marriage, voting, parenthood, opening a bank account, supporting charities and serving on a jury. Education should provide children, therefore, with the skills, attitudes and values to make them *good* citizens. The Act did not make clear exactly *how* these were to be taught, and much is taught through the example set by adults in the school, and the school ethos. A school can attempt to write its ethos down, but essentially it is how it is acted out in the day-to-day life of the school that is most significant to children.

In art and design, not only are the pupils made aware of SMSC issues within the *content* of the lesson and the subject matter of the work studied, but because of the way art is taught, children also develop an understanding of citizenship. This also applies to the 'arts' in general because they quite often involve pupils working in groups and, because the management of resources is so crucial to activity success, children have the opportunity to rehearse and act out their roles and responsibilities within the group. For example, pupils will have to share resources and take turns in using equipment. They will have to clear up after themselves, leaving a space prepared for the next child to use, not leaving a pile of unwashed paint palettes in the sink. Taking care of clothing by wearing an apron, and helping another child to tie the apron are the kinds of small ways that such responsibilities are learnt. Notions of citizenship, and our responsibilities to others within the community, are crucial in all aspects of education, but without a notion of responsibility to others creating can be extremely problematic.

Common ground

Planning

Central to all effective teaching, whatever the subject, is planning, asking the important questions, such as, 'What do I want the children to learn in this session? How can that learning be best achieved?' Clear, appropriate learning intentions, setting yourself and the children challenging, engaging and achievable targets, reliant on an understanding of the children's needs and abilities and the resources available, is essentially what teaching is all about.

First, know your children! Observation of the children's patterns and levels of achievement will enable you to find ways forward for them. It is sometimes assumed that assessment is at the end of the teaching process, but in reality teaching is cyclical, and identifying appropriate targets of achievement necessitates an understanding of what has been previously learned. Diagnostic assessment is, in fact, the first priority. This may seem an unusual statement in relation to art, craft and design. The idea of diagnostic testing is commonplace in English and mathematics, and virtually non-existent in the arts. Common truths, however, hold true across the curriculum, and assessing children's needs and abilities in order to design and target lessons appropriately is as necessary in the arts as it is in any other area.

Here are some key items to consider:

- **assessment criteria;**
- **assessment opportunities;**
- **balance of activities;**
- **capability and range of ability;**

- challenge;
- class management;
- classroom layout;
- differentiation;
- equipment available/required;
- expectations;
- extension activity;
- health and safety;
- homework;
- inclusion;
- information required for children;
- information required for helpers;
- learning objectives;
- learning outcomes;
- learning style of children;
- modes of motivating and exciting both children and teachers;
- National Curriculum Programme of Study references;
- number of children and their ages;
- other resources available/required;
- out of school activity;
- planning for development of ICT;
- planning for development of literacy;
- planning for development of numeracy;
- planning for development of SMSC;
- prior experience;
- prior learning;
- progression;
- recording and reporting;
- revisiting or reinforcement;
- sequencing of activities;
- teaching activities;
- teaching approaches and styles;
- time allocation;
- vocabulary;
- whole curriculum planning issues.

Planning a scheme or unit of work

A unit of work can vary in length, but will usually last for five or six sessions. It is crucially important for successful teaching not to plan single freestanding lessons (except in exceptional circumstances), but to visualise from the outset a sustained unit of learning with a theme and focus. You will see individual lessons planned by teachers for various reasons, but effective learning has to be sequentially planned. One-off lessons produce at best disjointed, fragmented learning and are counterproductive in relation to coherent learning. They do not provide an appropriate nor desired image of the subject. In effect it appears that you are using the time merely to occupy the children, not teach them something.

Teaching strategies

Effective teaching, regardless of the subject or organisation used, requires the teacher to be able to deploy a range of teaching techniques and teaching strategies. These will include the following:

- **assessing;**
- **demonstrating;**
- **diagnosing;**
- **differentiating;**
- **explaining;**
- **instructing;**
- **observing;**
- **providing feedback;**
- **questioning.**

Planned units of work, and the individual lessons within them, will identify which are the most appropriate strategies to use and this will hinge on progress made as well as on the particular nature of tasks set.

Primary teachers familiarly use a full range of teaching strategies in the course of their daily work. They should teach skills, techniques and knowledge very directly, allow differentiation by task and outcome, set work particularly pitched at the ability range and progress being made by individuals. They will use problem-solving approaches, allow experimentation and set exploratory tasks that are more child directed. They will allow self-discovery and facilitate children's learning from one another. By adopting a flexible approach to teaching and learning strategies, teachers facilitate as many avenues to the progress of children's knowledge, understanding and skills as possible.

Monitoring and assessment against learning objectives and targets

Children's attainment should be recorded at intervals throughout each key stage. At the Foundation Stage this should be completed and based on the appropriate area of learning noted in the curriculum guidance for the Foundation Stage for children in this phase of their education. Such records should be used to help the planning of future work and to form the basis for reports made at the end of each stage of learning. They can also be used for interim reports, for example end of year written reports and to inform parents at meetings during the course of a year.

Strategies for collecting data

OBSERVATION

In all aspects of teaching, one of the most important ways of finding out what children enjoy and can do is by watching them. Observing the ways children interact with each other and the materials, and set about tasks, is most revealing. By making brief notes as you watch them work, you will be able to assess their level of involvement, their thinking processes (to some extent), their skills in handling tools and equipment and their ability to work with their peers. It is best if these brief notes are made on small portable pieces of paper. If you put them on 'Post it' stickers or self-adhesive labels then they are easy to transfer to your **child profiles**.

DISCUSSION

Discussion in groups, or one to one, using careful questioning, can reveal the children's capacity to undertake the work set. Discussion is valuable at the beginning of a session, while the work is in progress, and at the end. Use questions such as 'How well is your work going do you think?' 'Why did you decide to . . .?' 'Which is the most successful aspect of this work?' These are open-ended questions that give the child the opportunity to explain his/her thinking and decision-making strategies. Children can also discuss their work with each other, and by listening to their conversations you will be able to assess their level of vocabulary and understanding of key specialist terms. Such discussions can be taped (video is best as it can be difficult to work out who said what and why on cassette recordings) and reviewed another time.

SELF-ASSESSMENT

The discursive questions posed above can also be given in written form. It is crucial that in whatever form is deemed to be appropriate, the child's perceptions of their achievements are sought and valued. Intrinsic to the process of learning is the capacity to review and refine the work done. Children should at all times be encouraged to reflect on their work, and working practices, in order to improve on them. This should go beyond preferences and relate to specific criteria.

PREPARATORY WORK

The work done in sketchbooks, planners and other places that records what planning, thinking and designing has taken place, are crucial sources of evidence of achievement. The final piece of work, be it a painting, song, dance or puppet has not come from nowhere, but is the culmination of a series of preparatory activities; it may or may not reflect the learning that has taken place. The preparatory work must be taken into account, looking for levels of sustained thought and involvement, exploration, experimentation and resource collection.

FINAL OUTCOME

The final outcome of a unit of work, whatever it is, will show evidence of what each child has learned, and what progress has been made, in terms of skills, knowledge, conceptual understanding, attitudes and values. This is probably the best reference with regard to the success of the learning experience. It is important to note that in the arts we use responsive assessment skills. Non-standardised outcomes, unanticipated learning, learning that surprises the teacher and the child are all highly prized.

Formative and summative assessment

There are two main types of assessment that you and the children need to undertake.

- **Formative assessment happens during a unit of work and forms part of the modifications to the learning experience; recorded as observation notes, reports of discussions, written statements and reflections, preparatory work.**
- **Summative assessment happens at the end of the unit of work and as part of the completion of the learning experience; recorded as the final outcome.**

These records provide evidence of the achievement and learning that has taken place. This evidence must be matched against targets and learning intentions, using focused assessment criteria to ascertain the progress that has been achieved. Schools often have their own formats for recording and evaluating attainment and progress. If you use published work schemes these are generally provided as part of the scheme.

Reporting attainment and progress

Reporting findings of assessment to children, parents and other professionals is always difficult when you first start as a teacher. The temptation is to bombard them with too much/little information, provide little/no analysis about what the assessment means, use too much education jargon, provide only a description of what the child has done, fail to explain that all is not lost and outline ways of moving forward.

Schools often have their own formats for disseminating information. For parents it is important that reports should retain a flavour of the individual child and not feel that they come from a generic word bank, i.e. prove that you know the child and value them as an individual. Always start with a positive aspect. Celebrate what they can do well as it is always too easy to criticise. Take care not to damn with faint praise and watch the jargon. For children just ticking work or saying 'good work' is meaning-less. Explain what they did well and what they need/could do to improve upon next time. For example in dance did they point their toes? In music did they stay in tune? In design and technology (D&T) did they plan and cut their material accurately? In art did they extend the range of their mark-making?

This then takes us back to the start, to the planning stage. Knowing where our children are and where they should/could be is at the heart of making us focus on our next activity or project with them and for developing the next spiral of our curriculum. Not forgetting, of course, that the evaluation of what we have done will cause us to develop the work that we have just finished, to make it an even more effective learning experience next time we do it.

Self-evaluation

As part of initial teacher training you are required to evaluate lessons that you under-take. The form in which you will be asked to record this will vary between institutions. This is not done to you as a punishment. It is done with you as part of devel-oping your ability to evaluate what you have done, why you did it and the consequent repercussions. The ability and confidence to reflect on and evaluate our teaching is a cornerstone of being a professional and constitutes the schism between teaching and merely instructing.

It is always important to evaluate how we are performing as teachers, no matter how long we have been a practitioner. Listed below are just some questions for you to think about from time to time.

- **How well do you plan lessons?**
- **Do you use a range of teaching styles?**
- **How is the pace and timing of your lessons maintained?**

- How good is your discipline, are you fair?
- What is your relationship with the children?
- How clear is your presentation?
- How well do you use your voice?
- Are children engaged and interested, i.e. what is going on when they are not?
- Do you spread your attention throughout the class?
- At what time of day do you perform best?
- Do you create a good learning environment and atmosphere?
- Do you make effective use of assessment and feedback?
- Are your lessons well rounded, with an introduction, middle and plenary?
- Is your classroom a safe, stimulating place for a child?
- How well do you share with and utilise resources with others?
- How well do you know your children?
- How accurate and useful are your records?

The implications of the Professional Standards for QTS for teaching arts in primary schools

All trainee teachers must achieve the Professional Standards as set out in *Qualifying to Teach* (TTA, 2002) to be awarded QTS. In the table below, the information in the first column is taken from that document while its implications for teaching arts subjects in primary schools are outlined in the second column.

1 Professional values and practice

Those awarded QTS must demonstrate that they:	Implications for teaching the arts in primary school:
1.1 Have high expectations of all children; respect their social, cultural, linguistic, religious and ethnic backgrounds; and are committed to raising their educational achievement.	Take account of the different experiences and influences that children bring to their learning in the subject area and promote 'learning for all' through coverage of the NC as a minimum entitlement as part of an inclusive education.
1.2 Treat children consistently, with respect and consideration, and are concerned for their development as learners.	Bring to their teaching the same approach as demonstrated in other subject teaching by overtly valuing the subject's contribution to learning in pursuit of educating the 'whole child'.
1.3 Demonstrate and promote the positive values, attitudes and behaviour that they expect from their children.	Consistently display a positive good role model for their children, e.g. changing into their PE kit, wearing an apron for practical activities in D & T and art and design, as they ask the children to do.

1.4 Can communicate sensitively and effectively with parents and carers, recognising their roles in children's learning, and their rights, responsibilities and interests in this.	Promote the subject to ensure children's regular participation, e.g. in ensuring kit and equipment is in school to facilitate this provision and by informing parents of their child's progress in their motor control/skills development.
1.5 Can contribute to, and share responsibility in, the corporate life of schools.	Engage themselves in extra curricular activities, e.g. setting-up and providing lunchtime or after school activity clubs that build on what has been covered in the curriculum time during the normal course of a school week.
1.6 Understand the contribution that support staff and other professionals make to teaching and learning.	Become aware of why the curriculum is like it is in their school, and to discuss this with the co-ordinator and other staff.
1.7 Are able to improve their own teaching by evaluating it, learning from the effective practice of others and from evidence. They are motivated and able to take increasing responsibility for their own professional development.	Evaluate and reflect accurately on their teaching skills in the area, and identify where further development is needed; access a range of relevant and appropriate sources of support for their work in the area, e.g. resources and materials to support their teaching, and to regularly engage in this form of activity to keep their teaching fresh and 'alive'.
1.8 Are aware of, and work within, the statutory frameworks relating to teachers' responsibilities.	Be particularly aware of the physical contact guidelines contained in the legal frameworks where a degree of this occurs, e.g. in supporting balance in gymnastic activities, or getting stance and position into place to effect correct performance of skill execution, e.g. in throwing overarm, cutting with saws. Be aware of health and safety and child protection issues, including legal frameworks; suggestions from professional bodies, e.g. DATA, NAAIDT, BAALPE and local policies.

2 Knowledge and understanding

Those awarded QTS must demonstrate that they:	Implications for teaching the arts in primary school:
2.1 Have a secure knowledge and understanding of the subject(s) they are trained to teach. In relation to specific phases, this includes: For the Foundation Stage, they know and understand the aims, principles, six areas of learning and early learning goals described in the QCA/DFES Curriculum Guidance for the Foundation Stage and, for Reception children, the frameworks, methods and expectations set out in the National Numeracy and Literacy Strategies.	Being secure in the subject knowledge base that will enable teachers to teach the subject effectively in pursuit of learning in and through the subject's various programmes of study. Specifically the physical and creative development needs of children in the Foundation Stage.
For Key Stage 1 and/or 2, they know and understand the curriculum for each of the National Curriculum core subjects, and the frameworks, methods and expectations set out in the National Numeracy and Literacy Strategies. They have sufficient understanding of a range of work across the following subjects: • **history or geography;** • **physical education;** • **art and design or design and technology;** • **music or drama;** • **religious education;**	Being fully aware of NC PoS, how they apply across both key stages, schemes of work, school policies and how this all impacts on planning to teach and delivering the content to promote learning.
to be able to teach them in the age range for which they are trained, with advice from an experienced colleague where necessary.	Improve their own teaching of the subject by taking opportunities to teach across the whole age range.
2.2 They know and understand the values, aims and purposes of the General Teaching Requirements set out in the *National Curriculum Handbook*. As relevant to the age range they are trained to teach, they are familiar with the Programme of Study for Citizenship and National Curriculum Framework for Personal, Social and Health Education.	Acknowledging that the arts, like all subjects, makes their own contribution to children's learning in these key areas and that all teachers require basic competence in these areas to teach effectively across two key stages.
2.3 Are aware of expectations, typical curricula and teaching arrangements in the key stages or phases before and after the ones they are trained to teach.	Familiarity with and clear understanding of NC documentation and QCA guidelines for the subject to assist with all aspects of teaching.

2.4 Understand how children's learning can be affected by their physical, intellectual, social, cultural and emotional development.	Take account of the need to provide for all abilities in children's experiences, including those with special needs and those who are performing beyond the expected level.
2.5 Know how to use ICT effectively, both to teach their subject and to support their wider professional role.	Know when and where ICT can support teaching and learning in the subject area, without losing sight of the fact that the arts in the primary school setting are about utilising a finite time resource and therefore must emphasise the practical and 'doing' elements above all else. Understanding of sequencing and progression in the subject area across the key stages.
2.6 Understand their responsibilities under the *SEN Code of Practice,* and know how to seek advice from specialists on less common types of special educational needs.	Familiarity with the Code, its implications for practice, and the applicability of adopting a range of strategies to provide for such children. How these factors influence the pace of learning and therefore building this into planning frameworks and teaching strategies to facilitate such differences.
2.7 Know a range of strategies to promote good behaviour and establish a purposeful learning environment.	Developing a range of appropriate teaching strategies that need to be applied.
2.8 Have passed the Qualified Teacher Status skills tests in numeracy, literacy and ICT.	

3 Teaching

3.1 PLANNING, EXPECTATIONS AND TARGETS **Those awarded QTS must demonstrate that they:** **3.1.1** Set challenging teaching and learning objectives which are relevant to all children in their classes. They base these on their knowledge of: • **the children;** • **evidence of their past and current achievement;** • **the expected standards for children of the relevant age range;** • **the range and content of work relevant to children in that age range.**	**Implications for teaching the arts in primary school:** Understanding of, and the ability to interpret, expected standards of performance using the level descriptors for the subject as a guideline. Have an understanding of the maturation characteristics children in arts subjects in order to assist planning and assessment.

3.1.2 Use these teaching and learning objectives to plan lessons, and sequences of lessons, showing how they will assess children's learning. They take account of and support children's varying needs so that girls and boys, from all ethnic groups, can make good progress.	The importance of on-going monitoring and recording of individual children's progress, and using this information to inform future planning and provision.
3.1.3 Select and prepare resources, and plan for their safe and effective organisation, taking account of children's interests and their language and cultural backgrounds, with the help of support staff where appropriate.	Being well organised, with resources (both motivational and instructional) in place to support lesson delivery, utilising where necessary the support of other staff and children where appropriate to do so.
3.1.4 Take part in, and contribute to, teaching teams, as appropriate to the school. Where applicable, they plan for the deployment of additional adults who support children's learning.	Planning as part of a team – from contribution to school policy for the subject, to discrete year group planning to ensure continuity and progression in learning. Ensure cohesion between long, medium and short-term planning.
3.1.5 As relevant to the age range they are trained to teach, they are able to plan opportunities for children to learn in out-of-school contexts, such as school visits, museums, theatres, field-work and employment-based settings, with the help of other staff where appropriate.	The nature of the subject and where it takes place automatically takes children to other places, but this can also extend to off-site learning potential, e.g. residential and field study work, museum and gallery visits. The arts and the consumer, audience, spectator. The arts in different cultural and historical contexts.
3.2 MONITORING AND ASSESSMENT **Those awarded QTS must demonstrate that they:** **3.2.1** Make appropriate use of a range of monitoring and assessment strategies to evaluate children's progress towards planned learning objectives, and use this information to improve their own planning and teaching.	**Implications for teaching the arts in primary school:** To inform planning, teaching and, fundamentally here, to use the statutory assessment procedures that are in place as well as devising personal systems for recording children's performance in the area to improve the learning experience of children.

3.2.2 Monitor and assess as they teach, giving immediate and constructive feedback to support children as they learn. They involve children in reflecting on, evaluating and improving their own performance.	The importance of built-in feedback to children on how they are progressing and the provision for children to contribute to this process themselves.
3.2.3 Are able to assess children's progress accurately using, as relevant, the Early Learning Goals, National Curriculum level descriptions, criteria from national qualifications, the requirements of awarding bodies, National Curriculum and Foundation Stage assessment frameworks or objectives from the national strategies. They may have guidance from an experienced teacher where appropriate.	Familiarity with the contents of this documentation and reflected in the activities planned and undertaken with children.
3.2.4 Identify and support more able children, those who are working below age-related expectations, those who are failing to achieve their potential in learning, and those who experience behavioural, emotional and social difficulties. They may have guidance from an experienced teacher where appropriate.	Planning for the full ability range and ensuring that more closely targeted work is provided for children at both ends of the learning continuum.
3.2.5 With the help of an experienced teacher, they can identify the levels of attainment of children learning English as an additional language. They begin to analyse the language demands and learning activities in order to provide cognitive challenge as well as language support.	Accounting for the need to ensure provision is made for all children and being consistent with the 'inclusion' principle. The role the arts can play in developing linguistic responses to experience and arts criticism.
3.2.6 Record children's progress and achievements systematically to provide evidence of the range of their work, progress and attainment over time. They use this to help children review their own progress and to inform planning.	Setting up of manageable record systems that are added to on a regular basis and which contribute to formative reporting procedures contributing to the summative assessment (see 3.2.7).
3.2.7 Are able to use records as a basis for reporting on children's attainment and progress orally and in writing, concisely, informatively and accurately for parents, carers, other professionals and children.	As above but for the purpose of formal reporting a summative form will be required.

3.3 TEACHING AND CLASS MANAGEMENT	Implications for teaching the arts in primary school:
Those awarded QTS must demonstrate that they:	
3.3.1 Have high expectations of children and build successful relationships, centred on teaching and learning. They establish a purposeful learning environment where diversity is valued and where children feel secure and confident.	Display the important teacher qualities of vitality and enthusiasm for the subject so that children look forward to their lessons, feel safe and secure in their activities, and gain from the experience.
3.3.2 Can teach the required or expected knowledge, understanding and skills relevant to the curriculum for children in the age range for which they are trained. In relation to specific phases: a) those qualifying to teach Foundation Stage children teach all six areas of learning outlined in the *QCA/DfEE Curriculum Guidance for the Foundation Stage* and, for Reception children, the objectives in the National Literacy and Numeracy Strategy frameworks competently and independently; b) those qualifying to teach children in Key Stage 1 and 2 teach the core subjects (English, including the National Literacy Strategy, mathematics through the National Numeracy Strategy, and science) competently and independently. They also teach, for either Key Stage 1 or Key Stage 2, a range of work across the following subjects: • **history or geography;** • **physical education;** • **ICT;** • **art and design or design and technology;** • **performing arts.**	Are conversant with the knowledge, understanding and skills required to teach effectively in the area.
3.3.3 Teach clearly structured lessons or sequences of work which interest and motivate children and which: • **make learning objectives clear to children;** • **employ interactive teaching methods and collaborative group work;** • **promote active and independent learning that enables children to think for themselves, and to plan and manage their own learning.**	Ensure continuity, progression and sequencing of input. Deploy resources and media that motivate and stimulate children. Deploy active, experiential learning tasks.

3.3.4 Differentiate their teaching to meet the needs of children, including the more able and those with special educational needs. They may have guidance from an experienced teacher where appropriate.	Acknowledge, and make specific provision for, all children across the ability range by: task, resources, language, feedback, expectations, etc.
3.3.5 Are able to support those who are learning English as an additional language, with the help of an experienced teacher where appropriate.	Seeing the arts as an opportunity for children to communicate through a movement vocabulary, as well as seeing opportunities to assist their learning of English as part of the vocabulary specific to the subject.
3.3.6 Take account of the varying interests, experiences and achievements of boys and girls, and children from different cultural and ethnic groups, to help children make good progress.	Becoming increasingly aware of what children bring to their learning from out-of-school activities and taking this into account in activity provision, i.e. assessing more than school-based work.
3.3.7 Organise and manage teaching and learning time effectively.	Developing well established routines and frameworks for delivery that maximise time allocations for the subject.
3.3.8 Organise and manage the physical teaching space, tools, materials, texts and other resources safely and effectively with the help of support staff where appropriate.	Teaching children about health and safety through the subject.
3.3.9 Set high expectations for children's behaviour and establish a clear framework for classroom discipline to anticipate and manage children's behaviour constructively, and promote self-control and independence.	Acknowledging the importance of providing very clear guidelines for children's behaviour as part of the safety needs that surround the subject's delivery.
3.3.10 Use ICT effectively in their teaching.	Looking for possible use of ICT to support the teaching of the subject without encroaching on the essence of the subject's active and practical participation elements.
3.3.11 Can take responsibility for teaching a class or classes over a sustained and substantial period of time. They are able to teach across the age and ability range for which they are trained.	As part of an individual teacher's proof of competence.

3.3.12	
Can provide homework and other out-of-class work which consolidates and extends work carried out in the class and encourages children to learn independently.	Encouraging participation in extra-curricular and related activities out-of-school, e.g. art, dance, drama, model clubs.
3.3.13	
Work collaboratively with specialist teachers and other colleagues and, with the help of an experienced teacher as appropriate, manage the work of teaching assistants or other adults to enhance chidlren's learning.	Build networks with colleagues in own school and beyond and begin to improve your own practice as a model for others. Work with curriculum coordinators, middle and secondary school subject specialists, advisors, business partnerships, etc.
3.3.14	
Recognise and respond effectively to equal opportunities issues as they arise in the classroom by challenging stereotyped views, bullying or harassment, following relevant policies and procedures.	Underpin the teaching of the subject with a fully inclusive principle always in play; relate subject specific learning to cross-curricular dimensions where possible.

Further reading

Key documents

DfEE/QCA (1998) *The National Curriculum Handbook for Primary Teachers in England – Key Stages 1 and 2*. London: Qualifications and Curriculum Authority Publications.

DfES/QCA (2000) *The National Curriculum Handbook for Primary Teachers in England – Key Stages 1 and 2: Update for 2000*. London: Qualifications and Curriculum Authority Publications.

TTA (2002) *Standards for the Award of Qualified Teacher Status and Requirements for the Provision of Initial Teacher Training*. London: Teacher Training Agency.

Useful websites

24 hour Museum at www.24hourmuseum.org.uk Provides public access to non-profit-making museums, galleries and heritage attractions in the UK. Funded by the Department for Culture, Media and Sport.

Africa Centre at www.africacentre.org.uk Provides a platform in Britain for African art and culture, and for news and views about political, economic and social developments in Africa.

Commonwealth page at www.commonwealth.org.uk Includes a resource for teachers of Key Stages 2 and 3, providing curriculum-focused information for each Commonwealth country.

National Curriculum Action at www.ncaction.org.uk Provides examples of children's work for each year group showing levels of attainment.

OFSTED at www.ofsted.gov.uk Reports of school inspections and reports on the work of HMI and government initiatives.

QCA at www.qca.gov.uk The National Curriculum documentation and guidelines for Schemes of Work.

Teacher Training Agency at www.canteach.gov.uk Documents available relating to the training of teachers.

Department for Education and Skills at www.dfes.gov.uk Provides information about education and skills matters.

2 TEACHING ART AND DESIGN IN PRIMARY SCHOOLS

Art and design

→ The importance of art and design
(adapted from QCA rationale for inclusion in the National Curriculum, 1999)

- *Art and design stimulates creativity and imagination.*
- *It provides visual, tactile and sensory experiences and a unique way of understanding and responding to the world.*
- *Understanding, appreciation and enjoyment of the visual arts have the power to enrich our personal and public lives.*

Pupils:
- *use colour, form, texture, pattern and different materials and processes to communicate what they see, feel and think;*
- *learn to make informed value judgements and aesthetic and practical decisions, becoming actively involved in shaping environments;*
- *explore ideas and meanings in the work of artists, craftspeople and designers;*
- *learn about diverse roles and functions of art, craft and design in contemporary life, and in different times and cultures.*

Personal values

Enter a school, anywhere in the country, and you are immediately aware of art. It might take a while before you know what the science teaching is like, or the school's approach to teaching history, but there, in the foyer of the school, will be children's art. The displays in the corridors beyond the foyer testify to the importance of the **visual environment** everyone in the school shares, and to what extent the children's artwork is believed to enhance that environment. Despite the immediate presence of art, craft and design, many primary school teachers will freely admit that they 'can't do art', or that it is too messy, or hard to manage with 30 children. Because art is on show and such a public activity, as well as being time and resource consuming, anxiety about the subject can often be high, especially in teachers who have little or no art, craft and design in their background and training.

Schools often have a paradoxical attitude toward the subject. On the one hand they will display work, and care enormously about the visual landscape of the school, but, at the same time, not invest in appropriate resources, or release teachers to undertake training. Art, craft and design, when it comes to funding, is often at the back of the queue.

Practical task

Learning objective: to look at the visual environment more carefully, and be aware of seeing.

- *When next in school, walk in the front door with fresh eyes.*
- *What colours are used in the entrance?*
- *Does the space look well cared for?*
- *Are there welcome notices for visitors?*
- *Is there seating for visitors?*
- *What else do you notice about it?*

In answering questions such as these you will make yourself aware of the visual environment of the school and the messages given by the school to visitors, children and parents. Even if you think you are one of those people who 'can't do art', you are constantly a discerning consumer of the **aesthetic** judgements made by others. You are **observing** all the time. Perhaps you have said the stock line 'I don't know much about art, but I know what I like!' What *do* you like, and more importantly, why do you like it? Reflect on that, and ask yourself questions about visual environments in other contexts such as shops and other people's houses. Why is your personal space at home the way it is? Why have you decorated your space the way you have with certain objects and memorabilia?

Also in the school foyer, notice what is being displayed.

- **Is there children's artwork on the wall?**
- **What kind of work is it (painting, printing, drawing)?**
- **Is it framed?**
- **Is there any 3D work on display?**
- **What impressions are you getting of how important art, craft and design is in the school?**
- **Do you think the displays are educational, i.e. to enable learning, or do you think their prime function is decoration?**

The question to be answered in this chapter is, how can you identify the useful art knowledge you have and use it to create meaningful learning activities for children? The important thing is to recognise that *you do have* useful art knowledge, and to approach your teaching from a positive rather than negative interpretation of your own capabilities in this subject area. When you got up this morning you chose what clothes you would wear based on judgements about **colour**, **line**, **tone**, **pattern** and **texture**, **shape** and **form**, concepts that form the main building blocks in art education, as well as employing notions of function and style.

Sketchbooks

You will need to record your thoughts and ideas, your observations, and the information you gain from the tasks in this chapter, and to do that you will need a

sketchbook. You may not have owned one before and are now beginning to worry that you are going to be asked to sketch, but don't worry. Think of your sketchbook as a journal, a diary, or a logbook. It is for **recording,** not sketching necessarily. Having recorded what you are learning in your sketchbook, you will be able to **reflect** on it. Art, craft and design, in common with all subjects, requires you to think if you are to understand what you are doing. The subject requires planning, decision-making, refining and many other **conceptual skills**, in order to progress. All this thinking is worked through in the sketchbook, either in words or images. It is your own, and personal, and need not be seen by anyone else, so you can include whatever you think is useful: photographs of displays of children's work, postcards from galleries, examples of fabrics, anything that prompts you to reflect on art, craft or design.

A4 size and with a hard back is the best choice. Some people like to keep a very small sketchbook in their bag or pocket so that quick thoughts and ideas can be entered at any time. A larger size can be both cumbersome and conspicuous, and until you feel comfortable using it, you may not want to draw attention to yourself in public! You can invest in a larger sketchbook when you feel more confident. So, buy yourself a good A4 sketchbook.

Throughout this chapter you will be asked to engage in practical tasks. You will be given information, but in order to learn in art, craft and design you need to try things for yourself and not just rely on what other people say. It is a practical subject and under-standing is often most effectively achieved through practical activity. The tasks are designed to both extend and make concrete any claims made, and allow the claims to be illustrated visually for future reference and reflection.

Practical task

Learning objective: to investigate a concept and record the investigations for reflection and reference in your sketchbook.

Let's look at colour. Over the next couple of days collect together anything that you think is blue: shampoo bottle, file, pen, jumper, jeans, scarf, bits of paper, sweet wrappings, anything. You will also want items that are nearly purple and nearly green (jade/ turquoise colours). You will want about 25-30 things in all.

Put all the items on a large table. It would be useful if you could do this task with a friend so that you can discuss your ideas together. You may have different views and will be able to help each other in making decisions.

Find the item that you think is the darkest blue and put it at one end of the table, and then the item that you think is the lightest (most white) and put that at the other end of the table. With the bits and pieces that are left you will be able to fill in between the darkest and lightest to form a tonal line. Put each piece down in turn, moving things around as you need to.

If you have difficulty in doing this, is it because of the shiny surface of some of the objects reflecting the light? Is it because some objects are semi-transparent and you can see the colour of the table through the object? Or is it because the objects are the same tone, but different in hue/colour? That is, the same tone but a different kind of blue, a bit more purple or a bit more green.

Put to one side of the line all the objects you think are slightly purple and put on the other side of the line those that are slightly green. You might want to use the diagram below to help you.

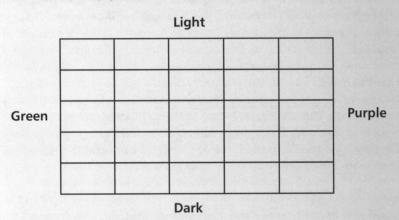

Which box would each item belong in?

You still may have problems with some colours because they are different in intensity, i.e. they may be **faint** with little colour in them at all, or **deep**, saturated and full of colour, and therefore difficult to judge in relation to the others. To complete this colour model it really needs to be three-dimensional to accommodate the differences in intensity, but for this task stick to two dimensions and make up a colour rectangle as the diagram above.

Having worked through this task you will now be looking at blue with more awareness and sensitivity. When you see two blues together you will ask yourself, which is the lighter? Which is most green? And be able to answer with some accuracy. In all art activity being able to see clearly and understand what is being seen is particularly important.

The previous task will help your skills in observation. Being able to observe carefully and clearly, both visually and through touch, is a vital life skill developed through artistic activity. It involves more than just looking, it requires being able to build a conceptual framework to which new visual and **tactile** information can relate.

Now you can see the differences in the blues you have collected, the next step is to **investigate** how to make them. What kinds of **media** does the average primary school have to help children make the range of colours you have found?

Practical task

Learning objective: to investigate various media and record findings for reflection and reference.

When in school, look for all the materials that could be used by the children to make different blues. For example: coloured crayons, felt-tipped pens, chalk pastels, oil pastels, wax crayons, powder paint, block paint, coloured papers of all kinds, and poster paint. They all behave in different ways and the colour they give is defined by the nature of the medium. Oil pastels, for example, will generate different qualities of blueness from chalk pastels. They are deeper, more saturated colours, richer perhaps. Using all these materials, and any others you might find in the stock cupboard, try to mix as many blues as you can, some dark, some light (adding white), some adding red to make them slightly purple, some adding yellow to make them slightly green, make sure though, that they are actually blue, and not purple or green. Record these colours in your sketchbook. Fill a few pages with different blues, either mixed yourself, or cut from magazines, and name them (bilberry, royal, French navy, sky, Pacific, parrot, harebell etc), and describe them verbally in any terms that seem appropriate to you, (sticky, thick, dusty, clear).

You will now be seeing blue much more clearly. What you have compiled is a visual dictionary, a thesaurus of colours for reference. Colours can be 'looked up' when a piece of work is being made. When painting a seascape, what kinds of blues, how dark/light/purple/jade, will you use (if indeed you will use blue at all)?

Impressionist painters were fascinated by the way we see colours in different lights. Monet painted many 'series paintings' (haystacks, Rouen Cathedral) looking at the same subject from the same angle, at different times of day, and capturing the different colours he saw on his canvases, as the light changed from dawn through midday to dusk. Find examples of these paintings either in a gallery or book, and include a post-card or two in your sketchbook. Describe the colours he has used. Are they the colours you would have expected? Place one of the images in the middle of a page in your sketchbook and try to mix the colours he has used, making a colour chart around the image.

Colours are considered to have a temperature. How warm or cool are the blues you have mixed? (Do not assume they are all cool, and some may be very cold).

Colours are also often associated with **mood**. When we say we are feeling blue, what do we mean? Do your blues indicate a range of emotions or moods? Are any calm, or threatening? Are any stormy or gentle? Record these thoughts in your sketchbook.

Expressionists are more interested in these factors. They are less concerned with the way colours *look*, but more concerned with the way they make you *feel*. Van Gogh, Mendleson-Becker and Rothko used colour to express their felt understanding of the world, rather than what they actually observed.

The activities you have just undertaken in relation to blue can be carried out with any colour. You could try another colour of your choice. You will find out more about colour in a later section of this chapter.

Creativity

Some teachers not only say that they can't do art, they also say that they are not creative. They think other people have more ideas than they do, and wonder how they can possibly teach a subject that is about developing the imagination. **Creativity** is not only necessary in teaching art, craft and design, however, it is a necessary part of all teaching. In order to translate useful knowledge into meaningful and appropriate learning activities for children in any subject, all teachers need to exercise what Elliot Eisner (1985) called the 'educational imagination'. Teachers have access to curriculum materials and schemes of work, but if the activities are to be fun and capture the children's interest, they have to be adapted and modified by the teacher, using not only professional knowledge and judgement, but also **imagination**. The NACCCE Report (National Advisory Committee on Creative and Cultural Education), published in September 2000, drew attention to the fact that not only is creativity inherent in all learning, it is necessary to develop confidence and self-esteem, and vital to meeting the economic and technical challenges of the future.

Creativity in the classroom is more about how we teach rather than what we teach. Thinking of suitable and appropriate activities in art, craft and design is no more or less demanding than in any other subject. The ability to be creative in teaching art, craft and design grows out of an understanding of the subject itself, and a clear notion of what you want the children to learn. Once you become involved in the subject and enjoy learning about it, the ideas will come as a natural consequence.

Creativity is also inherent in the aims of the subject. To engage in art, craft and design is to be creative in some way, and to produce something that did not exist before. The idea that artists sit and wait for inspiration (usually undernourished and living in an attic) is clearly a myth. Artists work at producing ideas, they do not emerge from the ether, but result from industry, developing powers of observation, practical skills and widening knowledge. The roots of creativity are based in careful observation and reflection. Artists are constantly looking and thinking about what they see, not only in terms of physical form, but also in terms of the human condition and the way it is acted out. These observations are recorded, in the main, in sketchbooks in both words and images. New ideas come from thinking about these things, and wanting to comprehend and express understandings of what is observed. Skills of material management are refined and influenced by other artists until some kind of artefact is produced. Once the artefact is made, an artist will often stand back and reflect on how successful they have been. The creative process seldom stops there. Usually an artist will already be thinking about what might be made next.

In school the process is essentially the same. Ideas are generated from visual exploration through various media, based on observation or memory. Imagination is the ability to contemplate something 'that isn't', but might be; contemplating something that currently does not exist. The imagination is developed through playful experimentation, and the interplay of thoughts and handling materials. Once children are involved in art making, they will often generate ideas as to what might follow or in what ways their work might progress. Children often make art at home, and their interest and enthusiasm can be fostered both at home and in school. Valuing art made in a range of contexts and displaying work in the classroom whenever possible will motivate the children to be creative and produce more. Also, by showing the children that you are working in your sketchbook and learning yourself, art, craft and design making becomes a joint learning experience.

Drawing

The 'I can't draw' syndrome has been a cross that too many primary teachers have borne, and for too long. It has completely unnecessarily clouded their vision and prevented them from tackling art, craft and design activities with any enthusiasm. Being constantly worried about their own drawing skills, and feeling they can do no better than the children themselves, primary teachers have often shied away from organising drawing activities. Drawing is a skill that has to be practised and rehearsed, in a similar way to playing a musical instrument or playing tennis, and, in the same way as playing tennis or an instrument, having a good teacher is an asset. It is perfectly possible to organise purposeful drawing activities for children, without being a great draughtsperson yourself. All that is needed is a clear understanding of the purpose of drawing and its value in children's learning.

Drawing is dependent, essentially, on two skills. The first is being able to see clearly and understand what is being seen, and the second is being able to use the **mark-making** material *effectively*. You will notice I have not said 'pencil', but mark-making material because you can draw with anything that makes a mark, whether it is charcoal, a finger in gravy or a stick in the sand. Neither did I say 'accurately', I used the term 'effectively' instead. I use the term 'effectively' because we have a motive for undertaking a drawing, and, although there are strategies and conventions in drawing, how good a drawing is really depends on the intention of the artist, and whether the intentions are met. For example, if the artist wants to record the experience of being on a pier on a rough and stormy day, strong, heavy relatively random charcoal or 6B pencil stokes may suit, whereas, if the artist wants to capture the delicacy of a sweet pea, the finest of marks from a brush and watercolour may do the job most effectively. Drawing is often a search for a **visual equivalency**, a search for a mark that, for the artist, represents an idea, a vision or a feeling.

Practical task

Learning objective: to explore the qualities of various drawing media. To investigate the nature of the marks they make, and to record and reflect on the outcomes.

Using any medium, those mentioned and any other you can find such as ink or wax, explore what marks it will make. You should use only black, white and grey media for this task because you are looking at the quality of the mark itself, and if you use colour you will be distracted by it.

Will any of the media make harsh spiky marks or soft cloudy marks? Will they smudge or blend or rub out? How dark and thick will they become, or how delicate and fine? Cover several pages of your sketchbook with this kind of exploration. When you have several pages of marks, go back over them and carefully reflect on the qualities of each mark. Add descriptive language to the pages (such as 'murky' or 'soft' or 'spiteful' or 'lively'). Decide whether any of the marks look or feel like something. You might have marks that remind you of a stormy sky, or a tree in winter. You might also try these same marks on different surfaces such as tissue paper, sugar paper or even paving stones. The surface affects the nature of the mark as well as the medium used.

Mark making is the vocabulary of drawing. The more marks you can make, the more effective a drawing can be. You may be still thinking of drawing as the process of making an image that 'looks like' the person, or still life or flower in front of you, and that what has been achieved through the last activity is all very well, but you still cannot draw a camel for the Christmas frieze. It is in this scenario that the distinction between being able to draw representationally yourself, and being a teacher is realised. If you are intending to teach art, craft and design well, the children should be drawing the camel and not you. Your role is to work with them using descriptive language, images from books or the internet (ideally, I would say go and look at a camel, but that may not be possible in the time available) and helping the children to determine what makes a camel a camel: the hump(s) obviously, the knobbly knees, the wide feet to walk on sand, the long eyelashes, the nostrils, the bottom lip, the quality of the hair etc. Through talk, exploration, practice sketching and careful observation the children will draw a camel freely and well and you need not, if you do not want to, actually draw anything yourself. However, you will improve your own drawing ability if you work alongside the children and learn with them by taking part.

Having worked through many of the anxieties primary teachers have about teaching art, craft and design in the primary school, and defined some basic principles in relation to personal attitudes and values, the following sections of the chapter clarify how the QTS standards can be achieved in art, craft and design. The nature of the learning process for you remains the same. Having read the information you will need to keep trying things out for yourself in your sketchbook and reflecting on the learning that is taking place.

Professional values

'Trainees should have high expectations of all pupils; respect their social, cultural, linguistic, religious and ethic backgrounds; and be committed to raising their educational achievement'

Children vary in their aptitude for, and disposition towards, art, craft, and design and this will be examined later in this chapter in relation to differentiation. It is the business of teaching however to enable children to learn, to help them come to understand the world they inhabit, and to understand themselves within it, no matter what their aptitudes or dispositions. Student teachers will often say that because they were not good at art at school, they were largely ignored as the teacher chose other children to do the stage set, or the display for the school hall. Indeed, some will say they have never had work displayed at all. You need to ensure that particular practice is not perpetuated.

Some teachers take great reward from working with artistically able children, while others will say that working with children who 'struggle' with art is the most rewarding, but this is not the issue. The issue is one of entitlement. All children are entitled to be taught well, and part of that, as will be discussed later under 'Progression', is that expectations of achievement must be high for all children, as teacher expectation is a key factor in children's achievement. It can be tempting, when a child has finished a piece of artwork to accept it, say, 'Well done', and put it away. What is more helpful for the child's learning, however, is to discuss it with them, to ask questions, to display the work so that it can be discussed further and with their peers, to articulate the successful and strong aspects of the piece, and identify those aspects that could be improved by further work.

Respect for children and young people *as young people*, entitled to every consideration that should be afforded to any adult, is fundamental to a strong understanding and working relationship between teacher and child. Children bring to the learning situation a wealth of knowledge and experience that is hugely valuable when teaching art, craft and design. They come to the lesson with stories to tell, experiences, understandings and questions, all of which are the substance of art, craft and design. Visual knowledge, understanding and literacy are shared across cultures and social groups and interpreted by them. Cultural diversity is to be celebrated as an enriching influence. In choosing to plan units of work on subjects such as 'woven fabrics', the work of people, mainly women, in a number of different cultural settings can be studied, raising the profile of the tremendous skill involved. Equally, using stories from a range of faiths and traditions as starting points for art, craft and design activity, and studying the art and artefacts of different faiths and traditions will broaden children's conception of what constitutes art, craft and design outcome and place it in relation to ritual and belief. Art, craft and design well taught can foster respect for others as effectively as any other curriculum subject because of the wealth of material available.

Practical task

Learning objective: to be aware of the wealth of material available to support teaching of faiths and cultures.

Make a visit to a museum. You will, of course, have been to museums before, but on this occasion take your sketchbook. Choose two rooms that you personally find interesting. It really does not matter which, what does matter is that you are interested in the material displayed. Make notes on what you see (types of objects, materials used, age, etc). Buy postcards if you can or, if you feel able to, make some quick sketches. What attracts you to these objects? How can you relay that interest and enthusiasm to children? You will be probably be teaching history, technology, religious education as well as art, craft and design. That is not a problem, it is an advantage because these objects made by artisans have a cultural/religious context and significance as well as being aesthetic.

Take time to see more of the museum to reflect briefly on how other material might be used, and make museum visiting a habit!

'Trainees should treat pupils consistently, with respect and consideration, and be concerned with their development as learners'

Often, perhaps because of anxieties about teaching art, craft and design, teachers provide closed activities for children, where the child has little flexibility to experiment or act independently. A lesson where the teacher has cut out shapes for the children to assemble might be an example, or when a group painting is devised by the teacher, rather than the children, and where the children are told quite specifically what their contribution will be. Personal ownership and individual direction is an inherent goal in good art, craft and design education, and a teacher needs to develop projects where children can invest their own ideas and thinking into the activities. Clearly you will plan activities within certain constraints. You will have limited time and resources, and you will have decided on the **intended learning outcomes** of any piece of teaching you plan, based on skills and knowledge the children should have and demonstrate. Also you will need to consider health and safety issues. Children need to share in, and understand these, if they are to become independent learners. They need to know what the intentions of the lesson are so that they are aware of their own learning. Equally, they need to be mindful of the dangers involved in using certain tools and materials. But crucially, they need to be set visual activities with problems for which there are a number of possible outcomes, and they need to wrestle with the problem to find their own solution. For example, a project on portraiture might include a session or two on facial expression. It would not be appropriate to ask every child to paint a smiling face. It would be better to talk to the children about how faces show moods, to talk about moods that they experience at different times and how that shows on their faces. You might want to show them paintings and pictures of gargoyles that show different expressions and talk about them, and then the children will be ready to paint their own portraits with their chosen expression, in expressive colours and using descriptive marks (as in earlier practical tasks).

Practical task

Learning objective: to resource a unit of work on facial expression.

Allow four or five pages in your sketchbook for collecting images from magazines or postcards from galleries that show facial expression. You will need to do this over a period of time, so set the pages aside and they can be completed over a period of weeks. A collage of facial expressions in your sketchbook could become the starting point for the children's research.

You could also set up a resource file into which some of the postcards you are collecting can go. A series of envelope wallets with topic headings is also useful. Ideally, all images should be laminated to standard A5, A4 and A3 sizes. This allows them to be stored easily, and keeps them clean when the children are using them. An image collection will prove to be a valuable resource in the long term. Anything and everything is useful. Cut up calendars at the end of the year, save greetings cards, logos, and anything else you happen upon, as well as exhibition catalogues. By mounting and laminating the images they will last a very long time.

'Trainees should demonstrate and promote positive values, attitudes and behaviour that they expect from their pupils'

The most important message you can give to children is that art, craft and design is to be enjoyed. It is the source of considerable pleasure and positive wellbeing. Making can also be a **therapeutic** activity. The very nature of some of the materials used gives **sensual** pleasure, clay in particular. A climate of positive reinforcement and value is essential. By not tolerating unkind remarks and careless behaviour, and recognising and rewarding positive comments, help and cooperation, children will eventually internalise your attitudes and enjoy the climate of the classroom. Linked to that is the need to be positive and encouraging, looking for value in the child's work, interest and efforts, to share the experience with them, learning alongside and taking part in the achievements. Wear an apron to show that you are in fact involved and working with them. It is very hard to enter into the spirit of art, craft and design if you are constantly worried that you are going to get printing ink on your clothes. It is also important to show the children that you enjoy art in the same way that it is important for them to know that you read for pleasure. It is equally important that you talk to them about gallery visits you have made and what you have seen. Sharing the pleasure of art making and appreciating can not only help you build a positive relationship with the children, but also develop in them a belief that engaging with art is a lifelong pleasure.

Also, children can work through issues and concerns by giving them form through art, craft and design activity. Young children, particularly, will freely draw worries they have, if given the opportunity, and can deal with them more directly once they have given them a physical form. A young child who draws 'my baby crying', and then throws the paper in the bin, may well be getting rid of the tension at home caused by a 'colicky' baby and her mother's tiredness, in a very physical and real way, allowing her to get on with being at school. Free drawing and painting space is an asset in any classroom, for just that kind of situation.

'Trainees should communicate sensitively with parents and carers, recognising their roles in pupils' learning, and their rights, responsibilities and interests in this'

Parents are not always the first to see the value of art, craft and design activity. The messages of the importance of literacy, numeracy, and scientific and technical knowledge are loud and clear, and art is seen by some as relaxation, or an extra-curricular activity. It is up to you to tell them otherwise, and convince them of the value of visual and cultural knowledge. By encouraging and valuing work done at home, by inviting parents and carers to come and view work, by taking photographs of the children engaged in art, craft and design, and of course through discussion, you will help them to appreciate the place of art, craft and design in their child's education, and make them aware of the life skills and values being developed.

Also, extra help is always needed; you could try to involve the parents and carers directly in the classroom, either as a classroom assistant or, more positively, employing the skills that *they* have. Does grandma knit? Does anyone sew or paint? Is one of the parents a craft maker, an architect, a window dresser, a dressmaker? All these skills and many more can be of real benefit to you as a teacher. Artists in residence are used in schools highly successfully, but on a smaller scale a parent with a skill, in a context carefully managed and designed by you, can have equal value.

'Trainees should contribute to, and share responsibility in, the corporate life of the school'

The first comments in this chapter related to display. In displaying children's work a school gives a clear message about the value it places on art, craft and design activity. The first activity in this chapter asked you as an observer to critique the visual environment of the school. As a teacher you are, of course, contributing to and creating that environment. You may wish to work with other teachers and the children in creating a mural for the school, either painted or sewn.

'Trainees should understand the contribution that support staff and other professionals make to teaching and learning'

Managing and carefully briefing support staff for art, craft and design is important. It is important also that support staff are not always asked to manage the art activity whilst you, the teacher, do the academic work. The surest way to devalue the subject in the eyes of the children and the parents is for it always to be in the hands of the classroom assistant and not the teacher. Support staff need to be aware of the learning intentions of the activity, not just what they are being asked to do. They, like the children, need to know *why* they are doing it, and have the educational aims clearly articulated. Appreciation has to be given also to their anxieties with regard to art. They may be experiencing all the anxieties you are, and more besides!

'Trainees should improve on their teaching, by evaluating it, learning from the effective practice of others and from evidence; they should be motivated and able to take increasing responsibility for their own professional development'

A recurrent theme in this chapter has been your reflection on your own learning, documented in your sketchbook. The level to which you undertake that reflection will indicate the extent to which you are taking responsibility for your professional development in this subject area. At the end of the chapter the short bibliography and website list will offer you ways to take your professional development forward. The National Society for Education in Art and Design (NSEAD) is the main professional organisation for art and design teachers in the United Kingdom and the contact details for that organisation are also given at the end of the chapter. The Society offers conferences, a research journal, a newsletter and a number of other benefits.

Knowledge and understanding

Knowledge of the subject

You may feel that you do not know very much about fine art, and are confused by much of what is celebrated as contemporary art. Perhaps you have read articles in the paper about the Turner Prize and find it difficult to understand what it is all about, and when visiting a gallery you are not really sure what you are looking at, or what to say about it. However, the assumption that unless you have followed an art course at some stage you know nothing about art is completely false. In reality no subject is entirely discrete or completely autonomous. Art, craft and design issues exist in virtually all other areas of human understanding and, as such, are impossible to avoid and no one can 'know nothing'. We are surrounded by visual culture and interact with it on a daily basis. Manifestations of art, craft and design are not only found in galleries and museums, but also in our personal, spiritual and social lives. Choosing a hairstyle or having a tattoo applied, for example, are undertakings propelled by a need to demonstrate style consciousness. A visit to a gallery, museum, or a particular building on holiday, suggests a desire to engage with art and architecture, and a trip to a DIY store is the precursor to time spent making in, and for, the home. Art, craft and design are functions of living and you know a great deal, much more than is immediately apparent.

Equally enabling is the fact that, whatever subject you have studied, the knowledge gained can be drawn upon and used to teach art and design. A degree in French, for example, may well have included modules on French cinema. Understandings of place and artefact to create narrative, and angle and viewpoint to focus and determine mood, will have been developed on such courses. Similarly, an A level in biology will have included careful observation of flora and fauna. Knowledge of this kind is valuable, and can be used as a starting point for artistic activity. A shift has taken place, to some extent, in art, craft and design education from formal approaches to the study of 'fine art', to post modern notions of interpretation, and personal understandings of visual culture and everyday arts, recognising the value and diversity of all visual activity. What might be deemed as valuable knowledge, therefore, in this cognate area is broad and inclusive and is rooted in the now and the commonplace as well as the distant and academic. It is important, therefore, that you approach the subject from a positive rather than negative interpretation of your knowledge.

Practical task

Learning objective: to explore the nature of current knowledge in relation to art, craft and design.

In your sketchbook carry out a brainstorm exercise using a spider diagram. Place the name of your strongest curriculum subject (history, maths, science) in the centre and radiate out from it the titles of key modules or topics that you have studied. Divide those into smaller units of knowledge; keep adding concepts and topics until you have filled the page. Then, with a different coloured pen or pencil, write over the top any connections you can make with any of that learning activity, and art. Some topics may be obvious, such as the study of shape and space in mathematics, others more obscure such as electronics. If for some, like perhaps electronics, you cannot think of anything, work with the links you can make and make those stronger and more explicit.

In developing this knowledge further, this section of the chapter will cover three kinds of art knowledge:

- **the basic art concepts;**
- **knowledge of art and artists;**
- **knowledge of materials and processes.**

This is then followed by knowledge of curriculum content.

Formal concepts

Several of the **formal concepts** in art, craft and design have already been mentioned in this chapter, and you will need a working knowledge of these concepts (sometimes referred to as art elements) in order to begin teaching. These formal concepts are: colour, line, tone, pattern, texture, shape, space and form.

COLOUR

Colour is probably the easiest to understand. In general in art, craft and design we are concerned with pigment, rather than light, and if you have any knowledge of science you will know that they are not the same. There are three primary colours red, blue and yellow. They are referred to as primary because from them (and white) all other colours can be made. Secondary colours are made by combining two primary colours (blue and yellow making green, blue and red making purple, and red and yellow making orange). Tertiary colours, brown and grey, are made from mixing the three primary colours together. The differences in the colours made depend on the proportions of the colours mixed. For example, when mixing blue and yellow, if a lot of yellow is used the colour made will be a lime/citrus colour, whereas if very little yellow is used the outcome will be more a jade or sea green.

Practical task

Learning objective: to pick up from the task concerned with mixing blues, and extend understanding of colour properties.

Draw a circle in your sketchbook to fill the page. Divide the circle into six sections as if cutting a cake. Over time collect from magazines and any other source scraps of coloured paper and sort them into six envelopes or small boxes (blue, green, yellow, orange, red and purple). Each section of the circle is for one of the colours listed in order above, so that if you start with blue because you now know blue well, you cut the scraps of paper into small pieces and stick them into one section being mindful that at one edge the blues will be more green, and on the other edge they will be more purple. Then, move to the green section and cut up the green scraps and stick them in their section, keeping the bluer greens next to the blue section and the greens that are most yellow towards the other edge. Next, onto yellow, and so on. When you have finished all the sections and stand away from it the colours should blend one into the next forming a colour wheel.

Complementary colours are those opposite on the colour wheel: red and green; purple and yellow; orange and blue. One is the most different colour to the other, and as a consequence the colours vibrate and resonate when put together. Harmonious colours are those closest on the colour wheel, such as red/orange/yellow.

LINE

You will have an understanding of a line, whatever your background in art. You will have drawn them hundreds of times. A line is often considered to be an edge, a mark that represents the boundary of one thing and the beginning of another. When you 'draw a line under' something, either actually or metaphorically, you are showing the separation of one thing from another, the edge. The line draws attention to that separation. For example when you draw a line under a title, you focus attention on that title by separating it from the text. The same is true in art. When a line is drawn it defines, separates and draws attention to whatever it is that is being drawn (whether that is an object, an idea or a movement). It gives it shape. Lines are then combined to form sketches, plans, and drawings of various other kinds. Go back to your mark making in your sketchbook and look at the qualities of the lines, no two are identical.

Practical task

Learning objective: to be aware of the wide variety of drawings and the part they play in communication.

Think of all the ways in which drawings are used, and find examples. Sketches are just one kind of drawing. Look for architect or design drawings, cartoons, maps, diagrams, signs, logos, illustrations and any other examples of drawings you come across in day-to-day life. Could the ideas be as effectively communicated in words?

Collect examples and stick them in your sketchbook, categorising them into informative, expressive, imaginative, technical and humorous.

TONE

Tone refers to light and shade. As light hits a solid object it casts a shadow on the object itself and on surrounding surfaces, causing it to be seen as lighter or darker in colour.

Look up from reading this book and look at an object near you. You will see that light (coming from a window or bulb) hits the object on one side. If the object has a reflective surface the light will be thrown back as a shine. The light cannot get to the other side of the object because the object itself is in the way, and therefore it is seen as darker. The intensity of the light can change, and this affects the intensity of the shadow, for example when your own shadow changes as the sun comes out.

Practical task

Learning objective: to become more confident in using marks to show light and shade in a drawing.

Put an object, a saucepan or teapot or something similar on a surface with a direct source of light (a lamp or a window). Look carefully to see how the light describes the object. Choose one of the drawing media you used for the mark-making activity, and use it to show tone. You need not draw the shape of the object on the page, just describe the surface in terms of tone. The tones below will help you.

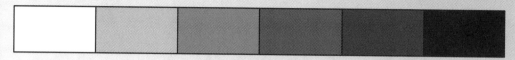

PATTERN AND TEXTURE

Lines, tones and colours are combined and repeated, either in a regular or irregular way to form patterns. The pattern of wood grain is irregular, but the pattern cut into a car tyre is regular. Patterns exist everywhere. Our fingerprints, trainer soles, paving and brickwork, pebbledash, wave marks on sand, leaf veins, stacked chairs, animal skins, tweeds and tartans are examples of both natural and manufactured patterns.

Strictly speaking, however, these are in the main textures. They are raised patterns that can be felt. They are seen as patterns and felt as textures.

Practical task

Learning objective: to bring together a collection of patterns for comparison. To record the patterns and textures for reflection and reference.

Your sketchbook can be used to collect examples of patterns. Take photos, cuttings and drawings of all the patterns you see. Ink up your trainer sole or finger and print the pattern into your book. Look carefully at the prints and patterns you have collected. Which are regular (organised, geometric) and which irregular (organic, freeform)?

Compose a regular pattern by combining marks in a formally organised way. For example:

```
=II=II=II=II=II=II=II=II=II    ><><><><><><><><><>
II=II=II=II=II=II=II=II=II=    ><><><><><><><><><>
=II=II=II=II=II=II=II=II=II    ><><><><><><><><><>
```

SHAPE

Shape is an area with a boundary. It is two-dimensional and individual shapes can be combined to form patterns. The area between shapes is known, quite obviously, as space. In terms of drawing, a shape is used on a two-dimensional surface to represent something that is actually three-dimensional in the world. The shape chosen either accurately shows the nature of the object (a flower for example), or a shape is chosen to symbolise the flower and be stylised and symbolic rather than visually 'true'.

The terms shape and space are often expressed together, especially in mathematics. Space however, just to confuse, is also used in three-dimensional terms in relation to form, and this will be discussed in the next section.

Practical task

Learning objective: to identify how shapes combine to form patterns.

Look back over the patterns you have collected and, using tracing paper if it helps, identify the shapes that make up the pattern. For example, a floral pattern may be made up of five separate petal shapes, five leaf shapes, a stem shape and the space in between, and this is then repeated over the paper or cloth. Do you think the shapes are representational or stylised? Take a simple pattern to begin with, and then try a more complex one.

FORM

Form is shape in three dimensions (3D). Most things that exist in the world have three dimensions and solidity, and the concept of form refers to the understanding of the space that an object, natural or manufactured, takes up in the world. From different angles and viewpoints any form will appear differently. The book you are holding exists in space and, because of its particular size and form, it occupies that space. Lift it into the air and look at it from underneath, and it changes, as it does when it is closed. Form and space are interrelated and are *experienced* rather than just seen. A photograph of a telephone box, for example, does not enable you to feel what it is like to be near or inside it. The photograph shows you the shape, and an indication of the scale, but again, scale has to be experienced to be fully understood. Form, then, involves a bodily, physical understanding.

SPACE

Space is what exists around shape and form, so space can be referred to in relation to 2D and 3D experience. In a sense, it is what is left. The depiction of 3D space on paper (a 2D plane) is a challenge to artists. When looking at a tree we see the branches, twigs and leaves, but held between them, and in fact divided by them, is space. The convention in north western Europe for the past five centuries has been to use the device of perspective, in an attempt to make a 2D image look as though it contains 3D space. In other parts of the world, and in much European contemporary art, the depiction of space in this way is not thought to be appropriate or even necessary.

Practical task

Learning objective: to clarify the concepts of form and space.

Put a chair on the table and walk slowly around it. Notice not only how the form of the chair changes but also the spaces defined by the legs. At certain points the chair will appear to only have three legs. Look underneath the chair and look at it from above. Imagine the rectangular box that would need to encase the chair for transport.

Being able to see an object clearly in 3D, and see the spaces created by it and around it, and being able to see size and proportion are valuable life skills developed in art, craft and design. The Cubists (Pablo Picasso and Georges Braque) were fascinated by the problem of creating 3D images on a 2D canvas, but were not happy with the convention of perspective. It was too 'realistic', they wanted to paint the *concept* of three dimensions, a problem they wrestled with for a number of years.

Knowledge of art and artists

Throughout this chapter I have referred to art, craft and design, and this section is no different. Knowledge of art and artists, craft and craftspeople, design and designers would be the complete heading.

There are three terms that are commonly used interchangeably in this context, but in fact they are quite distinct practices, and the terms need to be used accurately. They are:

• art history;
• art appreciation;
• critical studies.

ART HISTORY

Art history, as the term implies, relates to the knowledge and understanding of the period in which a piece of work was made. It includes the social, political, economic and religious context within which the artist worked, and any knowledge we may have of the artist's intentions in making the work. Much art historical information is now available to schools on video, CD Rom and the internet.

ART APPRECIATION

Art appreciation need not always have a factual knowledge base. It refers to the individual's engagement with the work itself, which can, and indeed often is, a non-verbal, felt response. Art historical knowledge can enrich and give depth to appreciation, and can prompt a sustained relationship with the work, but this is not necessary or always the case.

CRITICAL STUDIES

Critical studies refers to the debate that you have about the work. In talking to others, referring to various aspects of the work and comparing it with other work, your understanding of the work and the intentions of the artist are enhanced. In debating the work ideas and concepts are developed, often using technical and specialist language.

When viewing a painting in a gallery we are engaging in art appreciation. If we read up on the artist's life and the context in which the painting was made, we are learning art history, but if we then enter into debate with another person about the work we will be engaged in critical study.

It is important to be aware of the fact that virtually everything around you started its life on a sketchpad (an electronic sketchpad perhaps, but a sketchpad nonetheless). Virtually everything that has been produced has been designed, and the activity of engaging with art is not just concerned with da Vinci's *Mona Lisa*, Warhol's *Marilyn* or Emin's bed, the famous and the infamous. It is also concerned with objects and artefacts that inhabit our personal lives, such as jewellery, greeting cards and teapots. We are surrounded by objects in our everyday lives that not only have beauty and aesthetic appeal, but also emotional significance and economic value. Art, craft and design appreciation is as much concerned with our personal and intimate relationships with art as with our admiration and awe of the public and famous pieces.

Practical task

Learning objective: to illustrate ways we can articulate our understanding of objects, and identify their significance to us.

Choose an object that you have in your room. It might be a ring, or photograph or something from your childhood such as a toy or hairbrush that you have hung on to over the years. In your sketchbook do a very simple line drawing of it putting on the detail that has relevance. It doesn't have to be very large, but even a simple image is more appropriate than just writing the word down.

On the page, around or under the drawing, answer the following questions. If you can think of other things that are significant make a note of those, too.

1. *What is it made of? How do you know? Look at it carefully and describe its visual appearance. Describe the shape, form, texture, colour and surface decoration. Can you identify visual similarities or influences? (For example, in the style of Charles Rennie Mackintosh, or 'like the moon' or smooth as silk.)*
2. *Has it a use (cooking, wearing, holding plants)? Could it be used in any other way? Does it work well?*
3. *How old is it? Has it always been yours? Where did it come from? Why have you got it? Was it a gift? Was it handmade?*
4. *Is it a single object or part of a collection? Where do you keep it?*
5. *Does it have any personal, family or religious significance?*
6. *How much is it worth to sell? How much is it worth to you?*
7. *Why do you keep it? What makes it special?*

The last questions are the crucial ones, because they refer to significance and personal value. Simple personal objects help us create our identity, our difference from others and our place in relationships. A handkerchief given by a grandparent on a birthday can have enormous personal significance and value, while being meaningless and value-less to others, and perhaps never used as a handkerchief at all. Engaging in this way with objects, either owned by us or placed in museums, helps us give shape and under-standing to our lives and reasons for teaching art, craft and design in school. In recognising with children that so much of our daily routines are affected by objects and buildings that have been designed by artists, they can come to realise that being an artist, craftsperson or designer is not only a valid, but extremely important, career option, and challenges the notion that art, craft and design are merely pastimes.

Knowledge of artists, craftspeople and designers needs to be built up over time and cannot be easily accounted for in a book such as this. By going to galleries and museums, reading the papers and watching television documentaries, a body of knowl-edge will develop. If, every time you write a scheme of work in any subject, you consider the art, craft and design inherent in that subject, your knowledge will grow and develop, as will the resources you accumulate.

Knowledge of materials and processes

In order to make art, craft and design, children need to be made aware of the way materials behave. For example, if a particular piece of card is bowed, will it form a smooth curve or will it crack? When you did the mark making exercise, you were exploring the properties of wax and chalk, charcoal and pencil, and found that whilst they all could be used to make grey marks on a paper, they made very different grey marks. When you mixed colours you will have found that watercolours behave differ-ently from poster colour. You may also have noticed that the **ground** (the type of surface you were working on) also had an effect on the visual outcome. Thin kitchen paper (newsprint) is very absorbent and tears easily; cartridge paper has a smooth, strong surface, and watercolour paper has a rougher surface.

Many of the processes in art, craft and design are quite technical and you will need to experience them yourself before teaching them. For example, skills of batik or clay firing are not easily learned from a book, although there are many books on the market to give you advice and help you get started. To learn how to fire a kiln you really need to join a course at your local liberal arts college or adult education centre, but that knowledge is not necessary to begin using clay in the classroom. Treat clay as a material through which children learn about surface and texture and skills of modelling, and not as a material for making pots. Use the clay to enable the children to experience the sensuality of the medium and to think three dimensionally, do not feel that every time you use clay it has to become a final object and be taken home. Use it as you might use Lego. The children build with Lego, you take photographs of their creations, and they become part of an assembly perhaps, but ultimately the model is broken down into its component parts and used again by another child. Clay can be used in a similar way, which not only releases you from the worry of having to glaze and fire the work, but the cost of undertaking clay activity drops drastically.

Practical task

Learning objective: to use printmaking as an example of a particular process that involves knowledge of materials. It can be undertaken from a very early age and continued throughout life.

Prints are made when one surface is placed in contact with another and a mark is left behind (as you did when doing the practical task related to pattern). At the simplest level, a print is left by the sole of our shoe on the pavement after we walk through a puddle. Young children gain enormous pleasure from printing with their feet and hands, making their mark on the world.

You will need your sketchbook, some printing ink or paint, and a piece of polystyrene (from food packaging or a disposable plate).

1. *Trim away any raised edge to give a completely flat surface.*
2. *Make patterns and marks into the surface with a sharp pencil.*
3. *Coat the block with colour, either paint or printing ink.*
4. *Place the block on to a piece of paper and print.*

You will find that printing ink is more effective because it is thick and sticky and will stay on the surface, whereas paint will dribble into the crevices and not give such a neat finish.

Rubbings are also prints. To make a successful rubbing the paper needs to be as fine as possible so that it responds to the changes in the surface of the block, but not so fine as to tear easily. Wax crayon is an effective medium because it covers a large surface easily and does not smudge. Try using cartridge paper and pencil or charcoal. Is the effect as clear or effective?

Knowledge of materials and processes comes with experience. There are many 'how to...' books on the market, and only by trying (and perhaps failing at) different techniques will your ability to handle materials develop. Do experiment, that is what your sketchbook is for. It should record failures as well as successes. What is important is that you document *why* you think a particular process has or hasn't gone well, and the knowledge you have gained as a consequence.

Knowledge of the curriculum

In this chapter so far we have concentrated on *your* attitudes, values, skills and knowledge. In the following sections we turn our attention to the National Curriculum (NC) requirements for teaching art, craft and design in school. 'Art, *craft* and design' is the subject that has been referred to throughout this chapter, rather than simply art and design, the name given to the subject in the National Curriculum. The reason this rather more cumbersome title has been chosen here is because the National Curriculum has always stated (in small print at the bottom of a page) that the subject includes craft. Unfortunately, because craft is left out of the title and only exists as a footnote, it tends also to be omitted from both debate and activity in school. If craft is to take its full and rightful place in the art, craft and design curriculum, a constant reminder is needed. The subject is both visual and **tactile**. It is critical, conceptual and practical.

The National Curriculum for art, craft and design (1999) opens by making a strong claim regarding the subject's importance in children's education, and justifying its place as a foundation subject in the curriculum of the primary school. This statement, shown at the very beginning of this chapter, is very welcome. It clearly defines the important part art, craft and design plays in children's development. The prospect of being responsible for its realisation, however, can be daunting. Powerful statements of advocacy delight the informed practitioner, but the strong myths and legends relating to fine art and art education should not deter the untrained.

Practical task

Learning objective: to keep the National Curriculum statement in mind, and refer to it to support and clarify thinking about the role and place of art, craft and design in the curriculum.

Photocopy the statement at the beginning of the National Curiculum for art and design and stick it in the front of your sketchbook. Read it carefully several times and reflect on the tasks you have already undertaken to decide if, or to what extent, they conform. In what ways are the aims and objectives of the statement being rehearsed by the tasks you have undertaken?

Since the implementation of the National Curriculum, subject knowledge has been classified and presented, even to very young children, in a compartmentalised form. It could be argued that coherence and intelligibility has been sacrificed in order to attempt to show coverage of the subject and accountability to outside agencies. In attempting to ensure consistency, standardisation (if that is ever possible) and measurability, knowledge has been divided up. These divisions may have some meaning to adults, but they make little sense to young children. Children do not recognise the world in terms of subjects, but in terms of encounters and experiences, which eventually lead to meaning. Learning is holistic.

An interesting parallel can be drawn with the development of the art, craft and design document. Initially, in 1990, the subject had three attainment targets, which was clear and helpful in many ways, but when it was reviewed it was written as two; now there is only one. Gradually over time, as the documents were refined, it became clear that learning in the subject is seamless. Logically, the same should apply to all learning. The National Curriculum talks of 'links' with other subjects, but these are too often superficial and tenuous. What is actually required is a reunification of knowledge and understanding, with real and direct experiences at the heart. Fortunately the documentation for art, craft and design has been written in such a way as to allow for personal interpretation, and for teachers to be able to work to their interests and strengths.

Practical task

*Learning objective: to examine the **Programme of Study (PoS) for art, craft and design at Key Stage 1 and Key Stage 2.***

*Obtain a copy of **The National Curriculum, Handbook for Primary Teachers in England,** and turn to the section on art and design. You will now be familiar with the opening statement. Notice at the end of the statement the ' * Art and design includes craft' footnote. Read the four quotes at the top of the page. Which one, if any, rings true for you?*

Photocopy the next four pages and stick them in your sketchbook. Highlight the statements that begin 'During Key Stage 1 . . . ' and 'During Key Stage 2 . . . '. Read these statements again and identify the differences between them, by underlining them. Read the Programme of Study for Key Stage 1 and highlight the key words and list them in the space at the bottom of the page. Do the same for Key Stage 2. Again, identify the differences.

For example, under 'Evaluating and developing work' at Key Stage I, the verbs are to *review* and *say* (describe), whereas at Key Stage 2, children are required to *compare* which is a far more sophisticated process, looking for commonality and difference. Similarly, under that same section, at Key Stage I children are required to identify what they might *change* or develop, whereas at Key Stage 2 they are actually expected to *adapt* their work, and then look for further developments. In identifying these key differences, it is clear how teachers' expectations of the children need to increase from one key stage to the next.

Are there any surprises in the PoS? For example did you expect that children at Key Stage I would be expected to 'ask and answer questions about the starting points for their work and develop their ideas'? When you go into school, find out whether this is actually going on, or whether children are just being given something to do. Do they have a say in the kind of work they are doing? Are they able to control how it progresses, or does the teacher guide them quite rigidly? If the teacher is keeping a tight rein on the process, why do you think that is the case? Perhaps they have time or space constraints, or perhaps they are worried about disruption and mess in the classroom. These constraints are practical and to some extent understandable, but in placing further constraints on the children in the way they work, they will inevitably restrict the learning opportunity potential.

You will need, at some stage, to observe at least one art, craft and design lesson, and reflect on the extent to which 'the letter of the law', and the spirit of the National Curriculum, are being adhered to.

Schemes of work

Early documents had greater detail and exemplar material, and heated debates amongst teachers and academics illustrated that any list of examples shows bias and preference, and that leaving the interpretation and detail to the professional discretion of the teacher allows for diversity and regional priorities to be exercised. For the specialist teacher that is completely appropriate, but for the non-specialist and beginning teacher, the lack of detail can be problematic; it can be difficult to know where to start. For that reason the non-statutory QCA schemes of work (SoW) have been written and offer some direction to those who feel they need it. They are not, in fact, schemes of work as they are not groups of lesson plans, but they do offer a framework from which a scheme of work can be written.

Obtain a copy of *A Scheme of Work for Key Stages 1 and 2, Art and Design* (2000). You may have discussed the nature of a scheme of work in other subjects, and recognise that a SoW is a unit of planning for learning, developed using the National Curriculum PoS. The published schemes are not compulsory, but guidelines to show how the subject might be taught. Teachers can, and indeed do, develop their own schemes relating to local galleries or other resources, and design them according to their own particular interests and skills.

The DfES document has a helpful introductory booklet and a series of A3 sheets each defining a separate scheme. The schemes are intended to be sequential, except for the one on visiting a gallery, museum or site, which can be utilised at any time in Key Stage 2.

As an example, look at scheme 3A 'Portraying Relationships'. The introductory paragraphs explain the aim of the scheme, where it fits into the overall framework of the schemes, and then identifies what it covers in terms of the basic concepts, art-making process, key vocabulary and the necessary resources to carry out the work. Read this carefully. Bear in mind that the scheme is intended for Year 3 children. The back page defines the context of the scheme in terms of prior learning and possible future learning. The double-page centre spread relates the programme of study for Key Stage 2 to actual activities.

Practical task

Learning objective: to familiarise yourself with the DfES schemes of work for Key Stages 1 and 2.

Transpose one of these activities into six individual lesson plans. What would you actually do with the children week by week, in order to achieve the learning outcomes identified on the right-hand side? Also on the back cover, are possible adaptations that could be made. You may prefer to use one of those ideas when designing your lesson plan.

All the schemes follow a similar format. Once you have worked through one unit, subsequent planning will become easier. Remember, these are not compulsory, only guidelines.

Cross-curricular links

The interrelatedness of knowledge has been referred to before in this chapter. In relation to the National Literacy and Numeracy Strategies, it is important to recognise that art, craft and design are related to both literacy and numeracy, and common learning opportunities can be devised. Looking at paintings is an excellent way of developing children's speaking and listening skills, whilst learning about the paintings themselves. Literacy and numeracy skills need a context in order to create meaning, and art, craft and design can provide such a context.

Use of ICT in art and design

Computers, scanners and cameras are now used widely and effectively in the primary school. Computer software is available, even for very young children, which enables them to create and design on screen. Computers are immensely versatile and have their own unique functions that develop artistic thinking skills. They:

- **are additional tools to help children produce and manipulate images, and play with ideas and possibilities for the creative use of materials and processes;**
- **extend the possibilities for recording, exploring and developing ideas for practical work in the form of an electronic sketchbook;**
- **make it possible for children to document the stages in the development of their ideas electronically, share this with others, and review and develop their work further;**
- **provide a range of information sources to enhance their knowledge and understanding of the work of artists, craftspeople and designers;**
- **extend the possibilities for sharing their work with others via e-mail or developing a school gallery on a website.**

Concepts such as overlap, rotation, reflection and composition can be effectively taught using the particular properties of the computer. Each of the basic art concepts (colour, line etc) can be explored on screen, giving children immediate visual outcomes. Digital and scanned images can be manipulated to develop ideas, saving images at each stage to tell the story of the evolution of the final image. A number of references are listed at the end of the chapter that offer further and more detailed information on using ICT in the context of primary art work.

Social, moral, spiritual and cultural education (SMSCE)

Art, craft and design are about **culture**, about a quest for meaning through making and reflection. Many concepts already mentioned here, such as creativity and imagination, are processes through which we may come to know ourselves, and explore our relationships with other people.

Cultures in Britain today are diverse, and you may be wondering how you will teach SMSC in a school with children from a range of cultural backgrounds. It is, actually, much easier to teach a class with children from varied cultural backgrounds, as each has so much to offer, particularly in relation to religious and cultural textiles and artefacts. Diversity is to be celebrated, and art, craft and design can be used both to celebrate that diversity, and to work through issues of racism and prejudice. Through the study of cultural artefacts, children can come to understand other people's perspectives, attitudes, values and cultural practices.

Practical task

Learning objective: to be able to recognise art, craft and design as rich sources of discussion in relation to SMSC education.

Go to a gallery, and take your sketchbook. Look for artwork that addresses one of the four categories of social, moral, spiritual and cultural. They are sure to be there. For example, look for issues of:

- *personal relationships (social);*
- *religion (spiritual);*
- *greed or abuse (moral);*
- *self-portraiture (moral).*

They all have a cultural context, but you may find pieces that have a particular cultural identity, a Japanese print, for example, or a felt rug from Tibet. In the same way as you did in the museum, make notes on the pieces of your choice in your sketchbook, buy a postcard if you can, and reflect on how these works might be used in school to help develop the children's understanding in terms of their social, moral, spiritual or cultural awareness, and make gallery-going a habit too!

Citizenship

In art, craft and design, not only are the children made aware of SMSC issues within the *content* of the art lesson and the subject matter of the work studied, but also because of the way art is taught, children also develop an understanding of citizenship. Art, craft and design making (quite often) involves children working in groups and, because the management of resources is so crucial to its success, children have the opportunity to rehearse and act out their roles and responsibilities within the group. In group discussions about their work, children need to be shown how to respond positively to other children's work, and to see the value of critical friends in the enterprise of learning. Notions of citizenship, and our responsibilities to others within the community, are crucial in all aspects of education, but without a notion of responsibility to others art making can be extremely problematic.

Practical task

Learning objective: to become aware of the ways in which the organisation of an art, craft and design lesson can contribute to children's growing notions of citizenship.

Plan an art lesson. You may not be able to carry it out, but jot down the outline of a lesson you might teach. Reflect on the 'climate' that you will set up. How will you allocate resources? Will you appoint monitors? How will you ensure that all resources are sensibly used and collected in at the end in a fit state to be used again? How can you suggest ways in which the children can be helpful and encouraging with their peers? What language might you use to enable them to be supportive of each other rather than unkind? This does not mean that you should not encourage criticism, but that the criticism should be helpful and not hurtful, and offer strategies for ways forward. And you will need to help them rephrase what they say.

Make a note of how the activity will help children to show their awareness of, and responsibility toward, others. List the attitudes and values you hope to foster.

You will, of course, need to ensure that you demonstrate these attitudes and values at all times, however exasperated you may feel!

Teaching

Planning, expectations and targets

In terms of this section on planning, it is important just to note that appropriate targets can only be set with some prior knowledge of the children.

The second point to make is that in a subject like art, craft and design, where an inherent aim of the subject is for the children to be able to work creatively, targets need to be set that are essentially open-ended. For example, a target might be that the children will make a wire sculpture of a circus figure based on the work of Alexander Calder. The type and complexity of the figure will depend on each child's enthusiasm and enterprise in relation to that target. One child may choose to make a juggler, adding beads and tissue paper to give the figure character. Another may decide to make a simple seal on a ball in two dimensions, and yet another, because she loves making fiddly things, may choose to make a trick cyclist with all kinds of detail. As the teacher, you create the opportunity for them to use their imagination and develop their skills, and the children take it from there, with you teaching specific skills and providing resources, images, helpful tips and encouragement.

That is an example of an open ended, expressive outcome, rather than a closed, prescribed outcome. If you decide that the children will all make a ringmaster, giving them a drawing of a ringmaster, exactly the resources they will use, and perhaps even going through it stage by stage with them, so many opportunities for learning, thinking, imaging, planning, designing and evaluating are lost, and at the end of the lesson all the figures look the same. Demonstration, of itself, is no bad thing and is absolutely essential for teaching skills, but to teach art, craft and design well, i.e. allowing the children to be artistic, and skilled designers, they must think for themselves, be conceptually engaged and responsible for the work. They learn through application. Identifying appropriate assessment strategies is crucial in this context, as the criteria adopted have to be sufficiently flexible to cope with the open-endedness of the task set (addressed in the section on assessment).

There is a place for closed target setting, and that is when planning a focused skill task, such as rolling coils for a coil pot. The desired outcome is specific and fixed, with no real room for creativity. Having learned how to roll a coil and construct a coil pot, and having investigated coil pots in a range of contexts, the children can then work in an open-ended way to create a pot shape of their own choice, decorating it and embellishing it as they choose.

The third point to make in relation to target setting in art, craft and design relates again to knowing the children, not in respect of their aptitudes and abilities, but their particular interests, and their social, religious, cultural or ethnic group. It is important that every child in the class can access the learning and identify with it. To involve and motivate children they need to be able to identify with the learning, and understand the context in which they are working, relating new information and tasks to previous knowledge and experience.

PLANNING A SCHEME OR UNIT OF WORK

As with all other subjects, learning in art, craft and design has to be sequentially planned. One-off lessons are disjointed and fragment learning, and are counterproductive in relation to coherent learning. When planning a history project on the Victorians, you will plan a sequence of lessons, each building on the last, with a clear notion of the total planning 'package'. The same thinking applies here. Your art, craft and design planning may be linked into the history project and you could look at the life and work of William Morris (1834–1896). His designs were used for wallpaper and soft furnishings, and he and his contemporaries in the Art and Crafts movement and the 'Bloomsbury Set' epitomise the era in very many ways. A unit of work on printed textiles, based on organic forms, repeat, rotation and reflection, and produced by hand and computer, would be one way of planning art, craft and design activity in a meaningful setting. The series of lessons might include a visit to the Victoria and Albert Museum, if you are within travelling distance, or any other appropriate collection.

Practical task

Learning objective: to be able to plan a sequence of lessons in the context of another subject.

From the information given above, and anything else you know about William Morris and his contemporaries (Burne-Jones, Ruskin, Rossetti and others), plan a sequence of six lessons, each building on the last, setting aims and learning outcomes, listing resources and planning your time carefully.

Resources

There is a wealth of possibility in resourcing art, craft and design activities, both in terms of the materials that can be used for making, and through accessing information on the work of artists, craftspeople and designers. Browsing through a catalogue in a school staff room is a profitable way to spend a lunchtime, as is looking in the school stock cupboard. List the names and addresses of suppliers in your sketchbook for future reference, and make a note of materials, tools and equipment that you had not expected to see.

Since the implementation of the National Curriculum for art, craft and design and the requirement for children to be introduced to the work of artists, craftspeople and designers, museums and galleries have vastly expanded their education departments, both in terms of staffing and educational materials. Most galleries and museums, even the smaller, local galleries, welcome the opportunity to work with teachers, and run courses both for teachers and children. They produce information sheets and booklets, and all now have websites for you to access information on line. The larger galleries have useful bookshops. NSEAD holds possibly the largest stock of art, craft and design education books in the country.

Monitoring and assessment

The assessment of art, craft and design in the primary school has had a confusing history. Notions of subjectivity have clouded clear judgement, and interest in the final practical outcome has detracted from the purpose of the exercise, which is to assess children's *learning*. The final outcome, the painting or pot or weaving, however attractive or eye catching, is only one measure of what the child can do, or has learnt from undertaking the activity. Learning manifests itself in a number of ways and evidence needs to be gathered from a number of sources for an accurate assessment of the child's capabilities to be made, for example what they say or how they behave. The most important thing to remember is that you will not be judging the artwork 'as art'. You are not training to be an art critic or gallery owner, but a teacher, and as such the task is to *assess the learning* that has taken place. The focus is on the child not the art. That said, the next objective is to be clear what it is you want the children to learn. What constitutes worthwhile learning in this subject, and how do you know when it has been achieved?

Practical task

Learning objective: to identify knowledge and skills for assessment in art, craft and design education.

List in your sketchbook all the verbs you might use in relation to 'doing' art. It is a brainstorm exercise, so write as many as you can and whatever you like, for example planning, drawing, sharing, trying, refining, looking, laughing. Keep going until you have about 25 verbs written down (they must end in 'ing'). Divide the page into three columns: conceptual; practical; social/personal. Then put the verbs in the column that you feel they best fit. Think about the verb carefully. What kind of activity is it? Is it a thinking activity? Is it a skill enhancing activity (which obviously involves thought), or does it relate to social or personal development?

Some verbs may belong in two columns, such as 'discussing', because some of the talk that goes on in an art lesson relates to the art, and is conceptual activity trying to develop thinking about the activity (for example two children debating whether the composition of their painting could be altered to give the subject matter a different emphasis), and some talk is social, developing interpersonal relationships. It could be argued that such 'off task' talk is unacceptable and should be stopped, but sometimes it is perfectly fine for children to chat while working in art, and you will learn a great deal about their lives outside the classroom. Other verbs, such as 'cutting', clearly go in the 'practical' column.

If these verbs are what children are doing when they are involved in art, craft and design, then presumably these are the activities in which we want them to become more proficient. We want them to plan more carefully, taking in all possible considerations. We want them to draw more accurately, share resources more willingly, explain more clearly, and experiment by taking more risks and evaluating outcomes more rigorously, etc. You have listed 25 verbs, but these lists are potentially very long, and you clearly cannot assess each verb after each drawing.

Look at your lists and identify the terms that are most important. In the 'conceptual' column activities such as observing, experimenting, designing and evaluating would seem to be key, whilst in the 'social/personal' column activities such enjoying, cooperating and persevering are obviously important. You may have others that you have listed in either of those columns that you consider more important. Identify them, and reflect on why you think they should take priority.

You will have a range of words in the practical column such as sewing, printing, weaving, modelling or drawing. All of these activities involve thought, of course, but essentially the children are rehearsing and developing a skill. If you were to use these verbs as the basis of an assessment sheet for recording children's achievement, the words in this column would be targeted to the focus of the project. For example, in a textiles project looking at and working from the work of quilt makers, drawing, cutting and stitching could be the skills: i.e. cutting more accurately, sewing more finely and with increasing variety of stitches.

COLLECTING EVIDENCE

Having set appropriate targets, planned a unit of work and identified assessment criteria, the question now arises as to what constitutes evidence of achievement. It is not possible or appropriate to assess each piece of artwork in a unit separately. The progress made over the whole unit is what matters. Teachers will sometimes assess the final piece of work only, but that is only one indicator of what has been achieved. It is like saying that a sum is either right or wrong, when really the child's knowledge and ability is often most revealed in the processes they have gone through to achieve the answer, whether or not it is right or wrong. In art, craft and design the whole unit of activity needs to be recorded and assessed. Evidence is gleaned in the following ways:

- **observation of behaviour and working practices;**
- **discussion with peers in relation to work or stimulus material, use of language;**
- **self-assessment, written and oral;**
- **preparatory work, sketchbook, collections, skills, experimentation;**
- **final piece, imagination, skill in material handling, interpretation.**

PROGRESSION

It is possible to visit a Year 6 group and see not dissimilar work to that done in a Year 2 class in another school. Progression is not always evident, and is certainly not standardised from school to school. It could be argued that you can paint a picture of your mother whether you are 4 years old or whether you are Whistler, so what constitutes progression in this subject?

- **Widening the context: moving from the known and familiar to the new and unfamiliar.**
- **Increasing the complexity of the task: setting topic briefs that are increasingly complex and require higher levels of skill and knowledge (e.g. prints with three colours rather than one).**
- **Raising the expectation of achievement and increasing independence.**

DIFFERENTIATION

Differentiation in art, craft and design is most often achieved through setting a task that can have a range of outcomes and children undertake the task at a level appropriate to their capabilities. (An example was given earlier in relation to producing wire figures.) Differentiation is also achieved through levels of language and support, particularly in relation to setting short-term goals. More able children can work independently and are self-motivated. Others need fixed, often timed, tasks providing a staged passage through to completion.

RECORDING ACHIEVEMENT

The chart below might be one way of recording achievement in art, craft and design. You will need to reflect on the type of evidence that will indicate learning in the four areas. For example, sketchbook work will hold evidence of exploring ideas, and a

Art, craft and design	Achievement record	
Name:	Project title:	Date:
Exploring and developing ideas	*Becoming more experimental, able to pursue an idea independently, collects resources ...*	
Investigating and making art, craft and design		
Evaluating and developing work		
Knowledge and understanding		
Work completed I. 2. 3. 4. 5.	**Further comments:**	

group discussion will indicate the child's ability to evaluate and review the work that has been completed. The section headed 'Further comments' may contain information about use of language, or behaviour with regard to perseverance or helpfulness.

Practical task

Learning objective: to bring together the information in this section of the chapter to review the planning, assessment and recording of a unit of work in art, craft and design.

Reflect on the list in the section below as sources of evidence for assessing children's work. Can you think of other evidence you might use? What kinds of learning might each of these sources reveal?

Let us go back to the wire figure activity discussed under the section on target setting. Having looked at the various aspects of assessment, how could that open-ended task be assessed?

- **Research, information gathering.**
- **Experimentation, exploring ideas.**
- **Planning and preparation.**
- **Comment, use of language and key vocabulary.**
- **Material handling skills/manipulation of the media.**
- **Complexity of the final outcome.**
- **Review and critique of the work itself and the working practices.**
- **Enjoyment and involvement.**

These criteria have to be applied in the light of *what the child has previously achieved*. Go back to the document *The National Curriculum, Handbook for Primary Teachers in England*, and on page 33 the attainment targets for art, craft and design from I to 6 are defined. Read these carefully, notice again how the verbs change from level to level, and when next in school ask your class teacher how they are using them to assess children's learning.

Class management

One of the greatest fears of teachers of art, craft and design in the primary school is the potential for mess and disruption! Fortunately children enjoy making and have an enthusiasm for art. All you need to do is think carefully before the lesson starts as to how you will manage both the children and the materials. Initially you may want to allocate the materials before the lesson starts, but as your confidence grows and the children come to know the systems and procedures in your classroom, they will be able to help set up the activities and clear up afterwards.

The skill lies in establishing good working habits such as always wearing aprons, always washing up, always leaving the art table/shelves tidy, always putting newspaper on the tables, checking the equipment carefully etc. Simple rules such as always putting paintbrushes 'bristles up' in a jar for storage will extend the life of the brushes and ensure they are fit for use. Similarly glue spatulas must be soaked in hot water immediately after use, and pencil and colour packs need to be checked to ensure that they have not become muddled. Even very young children can be trained to follow simple rules. Encourage the children to contribute to newspaper, wool and fabric stocks, and to bring in pictures from home that can contribute to your image store. In fostering responsibility and corporate ownership, you will also foster careful working practices that will make class management so much easier. Time spent in developing such habits is time well spent and (ultimately) time saved. Well-structured lessons and careful preparation are the keys to success.

Being involved in large scale, public work can be daunting, but children need the opportunity to work in a range of scales and groupings. If the idea of a permanent mural is too much, then working in chalks in the playground is a way to get started. The dynamic afforded by allowing the children to work in pairs or groups on a larger scale piece of work is exciting. They learn from working with each other because of the necessity of having to explain what they are doing, and the reasoning behind any decisions made. Forming design teams and craft cooperatives to work through a brief gives children an insight into the way practising artists generally work, and enables them to work on a larger project.

Work outside lessons

Any of the examples given in this chapter can be used for art, craft and design activities outside the classroom context and lesson times. School trips and journeys offer interesting and varied opportunities for sketchbook work, making collections, recording sights and feelings in words as well as images, and generally engaging with the experience visually.

The home is a rich source of art, craft and design activity, looking at family albums to investigate family likenesses and issues of portraiture, for example. Equally, bedroom decoration and the personal occupation of space by arranging possessions illustrate how art and design is 'lived out' in our daily lives and routines.

The school, the neighbourhood, the shopping centre, the park or playground ... the list of possible contexts is considerable. Design a shop front, a stage for the school playground, a reading corner ...

Inclusion

Teachers need to consider the full requirements of the inclusion statement when planning for individuals or groups of children. There are specific references to art and design in the examples for B/3c, C/5b and C/5c.

To overcome any potential barriers to learning in art and design, planning for different and individual needs is crucial. Some children may require:

- **alternative tasks to overcome any difficulties arising from specific religious beliefs relating to ideas and experiences they are expected to represent;**
- **access to stimuli, participation in everyday events and explorations, materials,**

word descriptions and other resources, to compensate for a lack of specific first-hand experiences and to allow children to explore an idea for themselves;
- help to manage particular types of materials to which they may be allergic.

Art, craft and design acitivity is a tremendous source of pleasure for teachers and children working together to produce a stimulating visual environment and develop visual awareness.

Teaching art and design:

a summary of key points

— *The work of artists, craftspeople and designers is everywhere for all to see, and significantly influences the quality and efficiency of our daily lives.*

— *Children are entitled to the opportunity to become visually literate, and engage with the designed world, cultural heritages and meanings.*

— *Professional development beyond the NQT year requires a constant commitment to learning. Participation on courses provided by the local education authority, museums and galleries and other professional bodies will ensure learning continues.*

— *Visits to galleries should become routine. Most importantly, be critically aware of the visual environment, and keep working in your sketchbook.*

Further reading

Key government publications

DfEE (1999) *Art and Design: The National Curriculum for England*. London: DfES/QCA publications (also available at: www.nc.uk.net www.qca.org.uk www.dfes.gov.uk. publications); other publications are available at these sites.

DfES/QCA (2000) *Art and Design: A scheme of work for Key Stages 1 and 2*. London: DfES/QCA publications (also available at: www.standards.dfes.gov.uk/schemes). A range of schemes are downloadable, including 'teachers' guide'.

SCAA (1997) *Art and the Use of Language*. London: SCAA publications.

SCAA (1997) *Expectations in Art at Key Stages 1 and 2*. London: SCAA publications.

Texts

Several of the following authors have produced other good books that would also be useful for reference.

Barnes, R. (1989) *Teaching Art to Young Children 4-9*. London: Unwin Hyman.

Binch, N. (1994) *Oxford Primary Art: Teacher's Resources Book*. Buckingham: OUP.

Clement, R. and Tarr, E. (1992) *A Year in the Art of a Primary School*. Corsham: NSEAD.

Green, L. and Mitchell, R. (1997) *Art 7-11: Developing Primary Teaching Skills*. London: Routledge.

Herne, S. (1997) *Art in the Primary School (Policy Guidelines for the National Curriculum)*. London Borough of Tower Hamlets Inspection and Advisory Service.

Mathieson, K. (1993) *Children's Art and the Computer*. London: Hodder and Stoughton.

Meager, N. (1993) *Teaching Art at Key Stage 1*. Corsham: NSEAD.

Meager, N. (1995) *Teaching Art at Key Stage 2*. Corsham: NSEAD.

Morgan, M. (1988) *Art 4-11*. Oxford: Blackwell.

Robinson, G. (1995) *Sketch-books: Explore and Store*. London: Hodder and Stoughton.

Sedgewick, D. and Sedgewick, F. (1993) *Drawing to Learn*. London: Hodder and Stoughton.

Stephens, K. (1994) *Learning Through Artefacts*. London: Hodder and Stoughton.

Taylor, R. (1999) *Understanding and Investigating Art: Bringing the National Gallery into the Art Room*. London: Hodder and Stoughton.

Journal

The International Journal of Art and Design Education (iJADE), Journal of the NSEAD, Corsham (address below).

Useful websites

National Society for Education in Art and Design (NSEAD). NSEAD is a useful source of information on all issues in art, craft and design education, and worth joining. Ring for details. The Gatehouse, Corsham Court, Corsham, Wiltshire SN13 0BZ. Tel: 01249 714825. www.nsead.org/search

The Arts Council of England, 14 Great Peter Street, London SW1P 3NQ. www.artscouncil.org.uk

J. Paul Getty Trust at www.artsednet.getty.edu/artsednet/ An online service developed by the J. Paul Getty Trust. It focuses on helping arts educators, general classroom teachers, museum educators and university staff involved in art education.

Art Education at www.arteducation.co.uk Over 600 pages of art lessons, art projects and ideas about teaching art. Written by leading art educators in the UK with primary and secondary teachers in mind.

@rt Room at www.arts.ufl.edu/art/rt_room/index.html A resource for Key Stage 2 and 3 art and design projects.

Virtual Teachers Centre at www.vtc.ngfl.gov.uk/docserver.php?temid=57 Art pages linked to galleries, web resources, UK art departments on line.

Grove Art at www.groveart.com Dictionary of art terms.

Web Museum Paris at www.oir.ucf.edu/wm/ Information about art and artists all over the world. This French site is useful for teachers at Key Stages 1 and 2 studying particular artists or themes. It is in English.

Museums and galleries

These are just a few of the galleries and museums in London. For details of museum and gallery services in your area, contact 'engage' (address below).

British Museum, Great Russell Street, London WC1B 3DG. Tel: 0207 323 8511

Contemporary Applied Arts, 2 Percy Street, London W1P 9FA. Tel: 020 7436 2344. Fax: 020 7436 2446. www.caa.org.uk

Crafts Council, 44A Pentonville Road, London N1 9BY. www.craftscouncil.org.uk

Design Council, 34 Bow Street, London WC2E 7DL www.design-council.org.uk

engage (National Association for Gallery Education), 1 Herbal Hill, London ECIR 5EF. www.engage.org

National Portrait Gallery, St Martin's Place, London WC2H 0HE. Tel: 020 7306 0055. www.npg.org.uk

Tate Britain, Millbank, London SWIP 4RG. Tel: 020 7887 8767. www.tate.org.uk

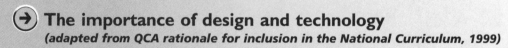

Design and technology

(→) The importance of design and technology
(adapted from QCA rationale for inclusion in the National Curriculum, 1999)

- *Design and technology prepares pupils to participate in tomorrow's rapidly changing technologies.*
- *Through design and technology, all pupils can become discriminating and informed users of products, and become innovators.*

Pupils:
- *learn to think and intervene creatively to improve quality of life;*
- *become autonomous and creative problem solvers, as individuals and members of a team;*
- *must look for needs, wants and opportunities and respond to them by developing a range of ideas and making products and systems;*
- *combine practical skills with an understanding of aesthetics, social and environmental issues, function and industrial practices. As they do so they reflect on and evaluate present and past design and technology, its uses and effects.*

Personal values

Design and technology (D&T) in its present form is a relatively new subject in the curriculum, both for secondary and primary schools. The label D&T is seldom used outside education but the activities associated with it cover a diverse range of professions, e.g. architects, chefs, designers (fashion; graphic; interior; landscape; industrial; product), engineers (mechanical; electrical; electronic; systems), town planners.

The Chief Executive of the QCA, David Hargreaves, in a major speech at the London Institute of Education on 'Towards Education for Innovation' 2001 stated:

> 'In the school curriculum design and technology has a notable place as a domain in which different bodies of knowledge and skills come together. Design and technology is not only a bridge linking the arts to science and mathematics in the interest of curriculum coherence; it is also a fertile ground for activities that support innovation.

> Design and technology is moving from the periphery of the school curriculum to its heart, as a model of the combination of knowledge and skills that will be at a premium in the knowledge economy, and it is from the best practice that other subjects can learn about effective teaching and learning for innovativeness.'

Don't you have to be practical to teach D&T?

The simple answer to this is that we all need to be (and always have been) practical in order to survive. We all use tools on a daily basis, some are simple containers, e.g. cups and kettles, others are more complicated, e.g. pens, telephones, cars and computers. Some tools take a long while to master, others are easier, but the amount of control and rate of expertise is dependent upon the individual. Whilst recognising that we all have individual talents and weaknesses it is not beyond the capability of any teacher to teach D&T.

If you have ever used any tool then you have the capability to teach D&T. Over the years a myth has been generated in our society that some people are just not practical. This is just a myth; it is worth remembering that practical activities have often held little kudos in the past.

Practical task

Learning objective: to reflect on personal practical experiences.

Reflect on your own experiences as a child and jot down the practical activities that you undertook in primary school, e.g. making a stuffed toy or making biscuits. How were you taught to make them? What amount of choice and control of the possible outcomes were you allowed?

Here are some of the thoughts that a group of trainee teachers remembered about the bookmarks they made as children.

- 'We were given a piece of material already cut to size. Then we had to copy the teacher's cross stitch pattern onto it ... mine got really messy, I couldn't get the hang of making knots and it looked as though it had had a fight with a cat at the end ... still my mum liked it ... I think she's still got it somewhere.'
- 'Ours was cut to size too but we were allowed to put on our own pattern. I did not like doing it very much as I couldn't think what to put on it to make it look interesting ... in the end I think we all just put on our names or initials in cross stitch.'

Figure I. Glove puppet making today

What is the difference between a craft or making activity and a D&T one?

It is fundamentally important to realise that just because children have manufactured something it does not necessarily mean that they have engaged in a D&T activity. The experiences that you encountered as a primary school child under the banner of 'craft' are very different from those that children should be experiencing today as part of their D&T work. However, just by looking at the products that the children produce you may be misled and think that this is not so.

In the past we may have told children in our class that they were going to be making clothes for a teddy bear. The children would then make the clothes for the teddy in question. The main rationale for the activity was to teach the children how to sew and to increase their digital dexterity to aid pen control and writing. The children were given pre-selected materials (chosen by the teacher) and the sequence of learning outcomes was closely laid down and controlled by the teacher.

Today we may still make clothes for teddy bears as part of a D&T activity. The fundamental difference is that the children will choose the materials and techniques for their construction. They will be set a problem and then be allowed and supported to construct their own answer with greater control of their own agenda and outcomes. This is known as **constructivist teaching** and **discovery learning** following the learning theories of Bruner (1960, 1966a/b, 1990) and Vygotsky (1962). This method of learning enhances problem solving in individuals (a key aspect of the requirements for D&T education) and aids the establishment of **intrinsic motivation**.

Much of what occurs in the classroom will look the same to the untrained eye. The teacher will still need to organise the materials for the children and give skill input sessions. However, there will be fundamental differences as to how these are achieved.

Another example is making a pencil case. In the past many teachers would have set the children the task of making a pencil case. Depending on the materials that they wanted to use (or more likely had to hand along with the associated tools and felt confident using themselves) the children would construct very similar (in size and shape) pencil cases. The emphasis in terms of assessment would have been the final quality of the manufacture of the case. There would be little design and that would be restricted to surface finishes. Today we are still concerned with the quality of the finished product. However, just as important is the process that child went through to produce the final artefact. You might identify a problem such as 'We have sets of colouring pencils that we need to store so that, as a class, we can use them quickly and easily. We also need to take the pencils into other rooms in the school and outside it for our art and design work'. This then leads to more investigation and modelling of ideas by the children. In essence you may still end up with the children making pencil cases. But the exploration of the problem and ways of solving it will be very different from the past (and each other).

Thus, the **scaffolding** provided by the teacher is instrumental to the quality of learning that can take place in the child's **zone of proximal development (ZPD)**. Such scaffolding might be:

- **asking a focused question;**
- **making a suggestion;**
- **encouraging or facilitating a peer discussion;**
- **sharing how others are/have tackled similar problems.**

This is not the sole domain of D&T, as the utilisation of **socio-constructivist** learning theories to provide for increasing intrinsic motivation in children aids greater levels of understanding and learning in all subject areas. It is vital to remember that the children are not passive, they are active participants in constructing their new knowledge and understanding based upon their past experiences and understanding within the social setting. Thus the social context, inter-communication, prior self-knowledge (and its self-construction) and prior skills influence the quality, range and amount of learning that can take place. As learning is a continuous process and often does not lead to a change in beliefs or conceptual changes it is a nebulous thing to quantify and evaluate.

You should now be beginning to see that the process of designing and making things is equally as important as the quality of the final product manufactured.

RESEARCH SUMMARY

There have been and will continue to be many different types of research into the way that children learn. The work of Bruner (1960, 1966a/b, 1990) and Vygotsky (1962) also highlight the social dimension and emotional aspects of learning (see Potter, 2000).

Key thinkers (and doers) in primary D&T are David Bartlex (2000), Prof. Clare Benson (1997a, 1997b, 1999, 2000, 2001), Prof. Richard Kimbell (1991, 1994, 1996), Rob Johnsey (1995, 1998 – a good practical guide and follow-on from this book), Ron Ritchie (1995).

Professional values

'Trainees should have high expectations of all pupils; respect their social, cultural, linguistic, religious and ethnic backgrounds; and be committed to raising their educational achievement'

As the teacher you will set all sorts of boundaries with each individual classroom, reflecting both your own and children's expectations in terms of work produced and behaviour. You are the standard setter. You are the guide and director of activities and standards. If you accept sloppy unfinished work from children then this is what you will constantly get. Set your standards high for all aspects of your class-work *for all the children*. Each individual will have their own capability for designing and making, but these are skills that can be taught. It is up to you to get the best possible work out of the children. OFSTED Inspection evidence (OFSTED 2002) has shown that designing in both key stages remains a weakness in schools, with expectations of children still too low for the more able child and particularly for children in Key Stage 2. One of the major problems with D&T activities is the length of time that they might take to complete. Thus children who are transitory, e.g. in local care, asylum seekers, travellers, etc., may start late in a project and even leave before its end. The engagement in a project that they know they will not be able to complete is extremely frustrating for any child. Special thought and care needs to be deployed in ensuring that children who miss part of a project can still complete aspects of it, get a sense of fulfilment from the activity and be working to their capabilities.

When you first start teaching it is difficult to know what is an acceptable standard of work and what sort of quality you should expect of children. The 'feel' for an acceptable standard comes with practice and experience. When starting to define your levels of expectations be guided initially by those around you in your school and government examples.

Practical task

Learning objective: to engage with the level descriptors for D&T.

When next in school look at the work that children have produced as part of a D&T activity, about two or three pieces will get you started. You need to have as much information about the work as possible and not just the final outcomes produced. With the National Curriculum level descriptors at your side try to work out which level you think applies to the work. Show your answers to the class teacher/subject coordinator and discuss with them your rationale for the levels that you gave. What were the surprises?

To help give guidance to teachers on the expected standards, the DfES has put exemplar materials on its website at www.ncaction.org.uk.

Practical task

Learning objective: to extend awareness of the government expectations of the level descriptors for D&T.

Look at one of the exemplars on the website (www.ncaction.org.uk). Note in particular the quality of the outcomes and the work that was done by the children prior to the manufacture of the final product. How do the standards here compare with work that you have seen in schools?

All participants in a D&T activity have a valued contribution to make. Whilst the scheme of work and lesson planning are the business of you the teacher, they need to be developed as a directorial role rather than dictatorial one. D&T, like art and design, encompasses all aspects of the curriculum and it too is an excellent and most appropriate place to explore and celebrate the diversity of our population.

'Trainees should treat pupils consistently with respect and consideration, and be concerned with their development as learners'

As with all lessons, during a D&T activity you are the one who is ultimately in charge of the class and its activities. Respect, as many have said, is not given but earned. If you set down clear guidelines and demonstrate these by your own behaviour then the children will follow. For some classes or individuals it may take time, but leading by example is the surest way of success. Children have a great sense of 'fair play' so however you set your boundaries for acceptable behaviour you need to stick to them. Children need a consistent response. This is all common sense and applies to all areas of teaching, but is easy to forget in the heat of the moment, particularly when you are stressed during a practical activity. For example, when cutting a wooden stick the child should be sawing downwards. If the teacher is then seen 'helping' a child by sawing sideways it sends out a mixed message and encourages children not to bother with sawing downwards as 'it must be ok 'cos the teacher did it'. It is always so easy to slip up in demonstrating good practice; stress caused by time constraints and lack of confidence do not help either. The best way is to get the children to act as health and safety guardians too. This makes them more aware of potential hazards and poor practice, giving them greater ownership of their own learning and understanding.

Practical task

Learning objective: to increase awareness of the need for children to take some responsibility for their own safety.

Describe the safety measures you have observed teachers taking when providing and delivering a D&T activity. Note how children's behaviour is intrinsically involved in the notion of safe practice.

Identify questions that would help the children to focus on safe and best practice.

'Trainees should demonstrate and promote the positive values, attitudes and behaviour that they expect from their pupils'

As previously stated, the children in your class will notice and pick up your attitudes and behaviour. If you enter into a D&T activity with reluctance and think that it is difficult or boring then so will the children. As with art and design, when engaging in activities such as food technology that require the children to wear an apron you should wear one too. It sets the correct example and creates a sense of bonding as a group activity. If you ask questions and a child gives you an unexpected reply do not just dismiss it out of hand if you are stuck for a response, record it on the board and go back to it later. This way the children can see that all opinions are valued, even those a little 'off beam'. Be aware too that if you 'borrow' a tool from a child without asking in order to help another one it will encourage some to follow this example!

'Trainees should communicate sensitively with parents and carers, recognising their roles in pupils' learning, and their rights, responsibilities and interests in this'

Many parents have an unclear idea what D&T is and how it helps their children to learn and understand the world about them. For most it consists of making things that will go home (sometimes falling apart on the way) and decorate the window ledge. Children are often not very clear at explaining to their parents what they have done at school and why. It is up to you to inform the parents about the activities that their child has engaged in; why they have done so and how this will help them across the curriculum. You need to do this by encouraging parents to be actively involved in the practical activities and by explaining clearly in reports and letters home. One very effective way of involving and supporting the community is the 'Feathers' (Family Evening Activities That Help Everyone Relax Socially) project. This Internationally recognised success is a Nottingham based after school club currently led by Pat Webster. Although only a pilot project it clearly demonstrates the benefits that can be gained all round by involving commerce, government funding, school and community support, expert advice and leadership and higher education together with the focus of D&T (Webster, 2000).

Involving parents in school assists the implementation of Inclusion, SMSC and Citizenship, for example you could involve the parents through coming into school and demonstrating the production of a meal that is related to a specific culture or religious observance. Discussion with the children may wander off to appear to be more of an RE lesson, but this does not matter. D&T activities are not abstract matters required for learning; rather they are interwoven into the fabric of our existence as individuals.

'Trainees should contribute to, and share responsibility in, the corporate life of the school'

D&T activities can permeate through the entire curriculum and support the learning of children in other subject areas. For them to do so they need careful and considered planning. Frequently PE, drama, music and art displays are 'put on' in schools to celebrate the accomplishments and work of the children and staff. D&T could be celebrated throughout a school a lot more. Displays have an impact and convey the ethos of the school (Bentley and Watts, 1994). In the entrance hall D&T contributions could be made through photographs of tasks undertaken by children or completed artefacts and designs. Generally more links with science using 'egg races' and problem-solving demonstrations could be made too. A good example of this can be seen in Samantha Leigh's work 'Lighting It Up' with a Year 3 class (Leigh, 2001).

'Trainees should understand the contribution that support staff and other professionals make to teaching and learning'

The use of other people to support D&T activities cannot be underestimated. Where possible include other people in planning and development of your activities. Do not just restrict yourself to your circle of friends, teachers and classroom assistants in school.

When you are fortunate to have assistance in the classroom make sure that the helpers (whatever their status) are fully briefed on the activity and on what their role as support staff for that activity will entail (especially health and safety implications). Where possible involve them in the planning, development and evaluation of the activity too.

It is important to consider the findings of OFSTED inspection reports, where in his annual primary subject report for 2002 Her Majesty's Chief Inspector of Schools (OFSTED 2002) noted 'In the best schools, teachers prepare short written guidance notes, drawings or demonstrations for classroom assistant and parent-helpers so that they all work closely to ensure consistency in their approach and make sure that learning objectives are achieved'.

Practical task

Learning objective: to be aware of the wealth of expertise and materials available to support classroom work.

Select either QCA guideline Scheme of Work Unit 1C Eat More Fruit and Vegetables, Unit 3b Sandwich Snacks, Unit 5b Bread or Unit 5d Biscuits (QCA, 1998). Identify a list of people and places that could provide background reading or information to support the investigation of food products in a primary classroom. Remember there are lots of commercial, civic and regulatory bodies that you can contact either through Yellow Pages or the world wide web! Hint: look at DATA, Nuffield and CRIPT, see Further Reading.

'Trainees should improve on their teaching, by evaluating it, learning from the effective practice of others and from evidence; they should be motivated and able to take increasing responsibility for their own professional development'

Regrettably many primary teachers in the past have had little in-service training and no initial training in design and technology, yet as class teachers they are expected to deliver all aspects of design and technology (Benson, 2000). Unfortunately for their future pupils this remains the case on many present Initial Teacher Training Programmes. In-service training cannot be relied upon either as it also has been shown by the Design and Technology Association (DATA) to be very patchy, rarely appraised and seldom planned for with the situation being far worse for courses related specifically to primary schools.

In an effort to regulate design and technology teaching DATA produced a two-tier system for design and technology competences for teaching (DATA, 1996).

- **Tier I contains the minimum competences required of newly qualified teachers trained to teach design and technology and for practising teachers to teach design and technology satisfactorily.**

- Tier 2 builds on Tier I and sets out additional minimum competencies for those newly qualified teachers trained as design and technology specialists, guidance on competences for practising teachers preparing for subject leadership and competences likely to characterise teachers who hold the post of subject leader in design and technology satisfactorily (DATA, 1996).

In this book we will be concentrating on developing those competences in Tier I. The self-audit in Chapter 6 is for you to record your own design and technology competences. It is derived from those laid down by DATA Research Paper Number 7 (Guidance for Primary Phase Initial Teacher Training and Continuing Professional Development in Design and Technology – Competences for Newly Qualified and Practising Teachers – with their kind permission) with a few amendments.

How can we improve standards in our teaching of design and technology?

- An honest and analytical assessment of what you currently know, understand and can do in terms of design and technology (Ritchie, 1995).
- Continue to build upon this personal profile of professional development through in-service training (Ive, 1999).

Practical task

Learning objective: to provide a visited competence for your D&T self-audit logbook account.

Write down an example of a product of quality that you have used. Explain briefly how it met a clear need and how well it fits the purpose for which it was designed.

Practical task

Learning objective: to record present competences in D&T and create a self-audit logbook account for future accomplishment.

Look at the competences on the D&T self-audit in Chapter 6 and start to fill in the evidence for work that you have undertaken. If you completed the previous task you can tick the visited column for part 4.3.4. This is an on-going audit and completion of it would not normally take place before the end of your NQT year. You should include all your experiences and expertise to date, even if you have not used them in the classroom.

Your D&T audit needs to be regularly updated, not only to build up a log of your competencies but also to help promote your confidence.

Remember wherever possible that sharing ideas and pooling knowledge with other people (not just other teachers/classroom assistants) at all stages of an activity will be beneficial and extend your range of knowledge and understanding. Having your capabilities verified by others will also help to increase your confidence.

Knowledge and understanding

Knowledge of the subject

You may feel that you have very little knowledge that is applicable to the teaching of D&T. We all have our own experiences and knowledge that can be used for D&T activities, and we will all have our own starting points. Do not be tempted to compare yourself with others; it will either depress you or make you complacent. You will at the very least be able to discriminate through analysis and evaluation. Every choice you make for any purchase of any kind relies on these skills. From the type and make of transport you use, what you wear, what you eat and drink; all these are value laden and require judgements by you.

D&T is a 'subject' that has no boundaries. There is no world expert and none of us knows it all at any one place in time and space. As you will appreciate technology grows and changes every day. This may sound rather daunting, but it should also be exciting. With designing there is seldom one right answer. Some answers may be more elegant, cost efficient, practical or attractive than others but it depends very much on the observer's viewpoint. For example, to decide which is most suitable to solve the need or problem you could view the designs from your own personal view, the user's view, judgement against specific criteria, the task brief or simply the majority opinion.

PROBLEM-SOLVING

When designing with young children it is best if they are given relevant solvable problems. This means that the problems need to be related to things that are important to them or that have some meaning. The teacher often initially identifies problems but even young children should be encouraged to progress on to find their own.

Practical task

Learning objective: to develop the skill of product analysis.

Collect a range of similar modern artefacts, e.g. shampoo bottles (with contents), teddy bears. Compare the artefacts that you have chosen. Try to identify:

- *Who is the intended user?*
- *What is its purpose?*
- *What material each is made from?*
- *How effective it is as a product (from different viewpoints)?*

At the lower end of Key Stage I teddy bears work well for this sort of activity in class. If you have a range of teddy bear sizes, shapes, colours and textures, all manner of extension can be done. For example, the question 'which bear feels the nicest?' could be the set problem from you as the teacher. The children then need to think of ways of testing the bear fur without being distracted by any other visual influences (fair testing with science links). If they get stuck then get them thinking about party games where they can only rely on touch (do not tell them the answer). If they suggest blindfolds I recommend that you do not tie one on a child. Instead take a towel and either get a friend to hold it in front on the child (so the child can back away from it) or let the child hold it himself with one hand. With a range of sizes the children could be asked to identify uses for each type of bear, e.g. very small ones to sneak into school or take to the shop as opposed to very large ones to snuggle up to when you are sad. Do not be tempted to use the children's own teddy bears. They easily get lost and damaged in the course of a day and some children may not have them or may have their treasure ridiculed.

You should now see that problems do not have to be complex and that with sufficient guiding (scaffolding) from the teacher the children should then be able to work through the problem and identify solutions for themselves. This leads increasingly to greater autonomy, with the children making decisions and being the driving force behind the activities that need to be taken.

Practical task

Learning objective: to begin to develop an understanding of the application of problem-solving activities.

Look at the key concepts for problem-solving as identified by Cy Roden (DATA website – expert tutorial) (Roden, 2001). How do these compare with the National Curriculum? Copy, cut and paste the 'teachers can' phrases into the relevant parts of your copy of the National Curriculum document for D&T.

DRAWINGS AND DESIGNING

Much of the information with regard to drawing techniques and developing your knowledge and understanding of mark making techniques is explained clearly in the art and design chapter in this book. However there are a few additions that are pertinent to D&T. Drawings for D&T activities are part of the process of designing and are used for a variety of purposes. As teachers we encourage children to do them in order to show and share with others what is going on inside their heads as well as to inform their designing and to help plan their making. Incidentally there is (and I suspect always will be) discussion on what design as an activity *is* and what designs in terms of models and drawings should be.

The National Curriculum encourages teachers to get children to 'design-before-they make'. Thus, these drawings should be representations of what the child wants to make. Often, however, these drawings have very little resemblance to their manufactured products. Very young children have particular difficulty in seeing the relationship between the design that they have made in 2D on a piece of paper and the 3D artefact that they want to make. Part of the issue is, as research has shown (Hope, 2000), that children in Key Stage I see drawings as an end in themselves, especially if they have had to grapple with the act of mark making itself, because most children want to 'design-as they-go'.

Figure 2. A Year 3 drawing for a hand puppet based on a tiger, drawn before manufacture

Figure 3. The manufactured puppet

Figure 4. A Year 3 drawing for a moving vehicle, drawn after manufacture

Figure 5. The vehicle in progress

Figure 6. The manufactured vehicle

SO WHY BOTHER WITH DRAWINGS?

Gill Hope in her presentation to the Design and Technology International Millennium Conference 2000 (Beyond 'Draw one and Make it' - developing better strategies for the use of drawing for design in Key Stage 1/2) sums up the reasons succinctly as:

> 'Realising that the task is bigger or more complex than can be visualised mentally and that external support is needed, whether from a drawing, a list or whatever, involves a level of self-awareness or metacognition which young children lack.

> Children are unaware of the limits of their visualisation skills. They think they have the answer and start to make something, leave it half done because it doesn't work or change it completely at a whim. By teaching children to objectify and record their mental images, visualise onto paper, we are teaching methodological efficiency for use in a whole range of contexts.'

Practical task

Learning objective: to compare work seen in the classrooms of different schools

Look at 'Beyond their Capability? Drawing, Designing and the Young Child' in The Journal of Design and Technology Education *Volume 5 number 2 Summer 2000 (Hope 2000), and 'Taking Ideas on a Journey Called Designing',* The Journal of Design and Technology Education *Volume 6 number 3 Autumn 2001 (Hope 2001) (also available on designdrawing.net/homepage.htm). How do Gill's reflections compare with work that you have seen or been a part of in school?*

Knowledge of the subject in relation to the national curriculum

What are the characteristics of a good design and technology activity? Design and technology contextualises creativity, curiosity, knowledge and understanding through the physical act of doing (Bartlex, 2000).

As part of D&T children are expected to develop their knowledge, skills and understanding of the subject through three main types of activity:

- **IDEA: investigative, disassembly and evaluative activities;**
- **FPT: focused practical tasks;**
- **DMA: design and make assignments.**

Where lessons are broken down into these components research has shown that there is a positive effect on classroom teaching.

Practical task

Learning objective: to explore the sensory qualities of materials (IDEA).

Collect together a range of different eating apples. Try to make the range as wide as possible. For each apple look at and record the following:

- *What is the skin colour?*
- *Is the skin colouring completely one shade or does it have markings?*
- *What does the apple feel like?*
- *Is it soft or hard to the touch?*
- *Is it shiny or dull?*
- *How large is the apple compared with the others?*

Now wash the apples under the tap and dry them with a paper towel. Remove the cores and keep the apples separate. Cut the apples into equal pieces with each piece retaining part of the skin. Put the apples on a plate and label each plate with a symbol, e.g. triangle, star, rectangle. Take one piece of apple and record the following personal observations.

- *What is the flesh colour?*
- *What texture does the flesh have? Is it soft, hard, crumbly?*
- *What does the apple smell like?*
- *What does the apple taste like? Is it sharp, sweet, bitter, tangy?*

If you conducted this tasting session with other people you should notice that each individual senses, feels and sees things differently (or remarkably similarly). These differences may only be slight but they are still there and are based on our own understanding and knowledge of the world through our previous experiences. If you were to try to record the same testing exercise with a large number of people (over a hundred say) then it would be very difficult for you to compare the sensory experiences because of the vast number of words that would be used. In order to reduce the complexity of this collation task in food technology we would use a **star profile** (in other curriculum areas this may be known as a radar chart) to record our observations with set adjectives to describe the apple (see below).

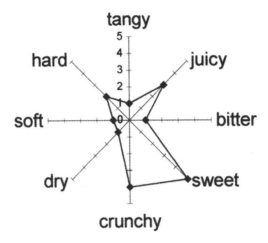

This addresses mathematics as part of collecting, representing and interpreting data for a given task (and for older children generating their own radar charts). This activity also links well with literacy, especially if you get the children to define suitable words to describe the apples. Indeed vocabulary extension should be integral to any investigative activity, where children should be taught to classify the words and distinguish between them. Children could also make a tasting booth so that their opinions and/ or notes are not copied, compared or shared until after the test (Ridgewell, 1992). This could link with the science requirements of fair testing and healthy eating and our bodies.

(For further details on food technology see *Working with Food in Primary Schools* and *Tasting and Testing*, (J. Ridgewell). Also *Food a Fact for Life* from the British Nutrition Foundation which has teaching packs for each Key Stage and computer software for Key Stage 2.)

Developed further it could lead on to the QCA guideline Scheme of Work Unit Ic Eat More Fruit and Vegetables (QCA, 1998). In this unit other possible IDEAs are explored such as:

- **investigating the insides of two contrasting vegetables;**
- **investigating, discussing and recording a wider range of fruit and vegetables.**

These then lead on to the FPTs:

- **controlling risks by following simple instructions;**
- **practising food-processing skills such as washing, peeling, squeezing and slicing;**
- **discussing and recording healthy eating through a pictogram.**

The conclusion comes as the DMA, which is to design and make a product for a particular occasion or group to encourage them to eat more fruit or vegetables.

Hopefully you can now see that if the children started with the DMA then the teacher would probably need to give the children most of the information before they could start. The children would be limited to a varied range of prior experiences and research evidence has shown that the quality and ownership of the outcome is significantly reduced.

Practical task

Learning objective: to reflect and compare design and technology activities with art and design ones.

Reflecting on your experiences in primary school, what do you think are the differences between a design and technology activity and an art and design activity? Think particularly in terms of IDEA, FPT and DMA. Jot them down.

Practical task

Learning objective: to reflect and compare design and technology activities with science ones.

Reflecting on your experiences in primary school what do you think are the differences between design and technology activity and a science activity? Think particularly in terms of IDEA, FPT and DMA. Jot them down.

One way of raising educational achievement nationally in D&T has been the provision of the QCA D&T schemes of work as guidelines for classroom activities (QCA, 1998 and 2000). The framework provides 24 medium-term plans called units that are all linked to long-term plans. Each of the units is designed to be taught over a term. The units have been broken down into IDEAs, FPTs and DMAs. Each unit is also designated for a particular year group. These suggested year groups and activities are simply guidelines and it is perfectly reasonable to make them more complex or simple to adapt to a given age range of children or capability, providing that you are aware of the National Curriculum requirements for D&T and can match them appropriately.

Practical task

Learning objective: to investigate the application of the QCA schemes of work and their relationship to the National Curriculum for D&T.

Look at the QCA schemes of work for D&T alongside the National Curriculum for D&T. Notice how the skills and designing increase with age, also how they develop and build upon each other. Look at how they also interrelate with other National Curriculum subject areas, particularly science.

The use of the QCA schemes of work (QCA, 1998 and 2000) as a general guidance for D&T activities in class should help you to ensure that your D&T activities are not:

- craft experiences with children making near identical products;
- excessively open-ended, requiring skills and knowledge beyond the capability of the children;
- set in isolation from the rest of the child's experiences in school and the National Curriculum;
- too prescriptive.

Remember, the guidelines are not written on tablets of stone, they are just suggestions, although most schools use them. As such they are best used when they are adjusted to the class that you have in front of you. Each group of children that you teach will come with their own previous knowledge and experiences; you will do them a great injustice and miss out on potential learning experiences if you do not make full use of these.

Having looked at the QCA Schemes of Work for D&T you may now be worried that you will not be able to teach some (or any!) of them. This is a perfectly natural response. Do not worry!

Practical task

Learning objective: to be able to modify an activity to make it D&T compliant, using prior knowledge and experience.

Select one practical activity that you undertook as a child in primary school or have participated in during a teaching block. Using the National Curriculum programmes of study for design and technology and/or the QCA scheme of work guidelines (QCA, 1998 and 2000) identify where such an activity could fit in. Jot down any changes to the activity that you would need to make in order for it to be considered suitable as a D&T activity.

Cross-curricular links

D&T makes an important and significant contribution to the National Curriculum's aim of promoting learning 'across the curriculum'. If you look at any of the main published schemes of work (i.e. QCA, DATA) you will notice that there are specific and pertinent links with all areas of the curriculum. As previously stated D&T activities are not abstract and esoteric. They are set in the real world about us based on values and experiences. As such they have much to offer as support and reinforcement for other subjects and aspects of our life.

> 'Concentration on literacy and numeracy should not detract from a balanced, integrated and reinforcing scheme of making activities that not only develops ideas, spatial perception and dexterity, but also problem-solving and related analytic, language and numeracy skills'. (Eggleston, 2000).

Social, moral, spiritual and cultural education (SMSC)

The child who dislikes a D&T lesson is a very rare person. The main reason why children like D&T lessons is that they can learn a great deal without even being aware of it. D&T can be stimulating and demanding for the whole capability range. Because of the social nature of D&T activities it should (as with the other arts) be a key player in the development of the 'whole child'. Thus they need through D&T to develop social skills, be made aware of their moral obligations and have reference to their own and others' cultural identities (and requirements). The spiritual element will come through the development of their creative capacity.

In essence, D&T provides opportunities to promote:

- *social development*, **through helping children recognise the need to consider the views of others when discussing design ideas (e.g. working together with others to solve problems, developing ideas by sharing and pooling talents and information);**
- *moral development*, **through helping children to reflect on how technology affects the environment so they can make informed choices when designing and making; and through discussing the moral dilemmas posed by introducing new technologies within different values systems and the advantages and disadvantages of new technology to local, national and global communities (e.g. comparing the use of veneers for furniture rather than solid timber reduces the number of hardwood trees that are needed for production);**
- *spiritual development*, **through helping children recognise their own creativity and the creativity of others in finding solutions to problems, and through recognising the tension between material and non-material needs (e.g. consider the aesthetic appeal of an artefact as well as its function, how does it make you feel?);**
- *cultural development*, **through exploring the contribution of products to the quality of life within different cultures, and through valuing and reflecting on the responses of people from other cultures to design solutions (e.g. looking at artefacts made from recycled materials where access to resources is scarce - tin cans into light shades; animal hides into coats; mulch to improve garden soil quality on over processed land).**

(Taken from design and technology – The National Curriculum for England, 1999 where other examples are given.)

Use of ICT

More primary schools are using ICT to support primary D&T activities (OFSTED, 2002). This is a positive step forward but there has been little movement forward in the use of ICT as a control device since the work of Prichard (1997), which is a shame because there are some good examples and support materials available (see CRIPT and DATA support materials and publications). DATA (1995a, 1996a, 1996b) has outlined three specific uses of ICT in D&T as follows.

AS A KNOWLEDGE SOURCE

Using CD-Roms to:

- give access to unlimited amounts of information (e.g. using a **CD-Rom** encyclopaedia to find out about other times/cultures);
- support designing and making (e.g. to show how manufacturers and designers use **ICT in industry**);
- allow extraction (e.g. collecting data from data bases to integrate with the child's own work);
- stimulate discussion and evaluation (e.g. using questionnaires and resulting charts to indicate preferences).

AS A TOOL

For:

- researching information (e.g. using the world wide web to conduct information gathering on a topic);
- analysing information (e.g. looking up nutritional information and relating it to their diet);
- presenting information (e.g. using desk top publishing programmes to present a design idea);
- modelling (e.g. using drawing and painting programmes to model ideas);
- manufacturing (e.g. using devices such as a printer to produce a net for a package to contain biscuits; a sewing machine to produce a pattern designed on a drawing package).

AS A COMPONENT

- control (e.g. using a floor turtle, designing a route for a buggy to move along, switches for model houses, flow charts, controlling simple devices).

Teaching

Planning, expectations and targets

As with all teaching the main ingredient for good D&T teaching is planning. It is not possible to teach an effective D&T activity 'on the hoof'. Some activities may seem incredibly simple, but if you want the children to really learn from the experience and be able to extend themselves to their potential, then detailed planning is required.

As mentioned in the introduction it is not appropriate to plan individual lesson/activities for D&T. More appropriately at the beginning of your teaching career you would be planning and developing a teaching pack to support a unit of work. An example of what this means in practice is exemplified by Carolyn McGee with her Year 3 class (McGee, 2000). Here you can see how she worked with government documents applying the requirements to the children in front of her.

Practical task

Learning objective: to develop an awareness of health and safety issues.

Look at the planning and subsequent developing that Carolyn did (McGee, 2000). Notice how she dealt with the health and safety aspects of the stapler. What other health and safety aspects would she have needed to plan? It is important to note that assessment was very much part of her planning process. How does this compare with plans that you have made or used?

Significant case studies and research conducted by Kyriacou (1991) and Ritchie (2001) have identified many key aspects that lead to a productive primary D&T environment.

The classroom

- A well organised classroom with resources clearly labelled and easily available.
- The classroom is appropriately prepared for practical activities before the children arrive.
- Ensuring that the children have an adequate range of (and opportunity to use) materials and tools when designing and making.
- Ensuring appropriate space for activities and demarcation of them during the activity.

Other adults

- Helpers are included in the development and planning of activities.
- Helpers are briefed on the activity and their role as support staff for that activity.
- Sharing ideas and pooling knowledge with other people (not just other teachers/ classroom assistants) at all stages of the activity.

Health and safety

- Appropriate risk assessment and suitable precautions for practical work have been undertaken.
- Planned effective management strategies in handling child movement and the general level of noise when engaged in practical work.

Interventions

- Questions.
- Pre-planned interventions to improve confidence are included.
- Pre-planned interventions to help children to progress are included.
- Thinking twice before intervening with children in difficulties and then guiding rather than doing the task for them.

Differentiation and assessment

- Careful thought given in planning to differentiate activities and to encourage children's input.
- Considered formative as well as summative assessment of individual children's current understanding and skills.
- Planning time to reflect during the activity, allowing children to pause and ponder.
- Planning time for teacher observation and reflection during the activity.
- Setting starting points in appropriate contexts that are stimulating and relevant. Wherever possible these should relate to other areas of the curriculum to reinforce learning and meaning.

Learning outcomes

- Clearly defined educational objectives that take appropriate account of children's needs, particularly in terms of their capabilities, interests, motivation, the context of the lesson, the work they have previously done and will do in the future as part of their programmes of study.

Monitoring and assessment

There is a statutory requirement for children to be teacher assessed at the end of each key stage in D&T (no National Curriculum Test yet!). Thus, assessment in D&T is based upon the teacher's appraisal of where they think the work that the child has produced 'best fits' the level descriptors as given by the National Curriculum orders (Kimbell, 1994).

There is also a requirement that you ensure that work in D&T for all children meets the National Curriculum requirements and has breadth, balance and progression and that you report at least annually to parents on their child's progress and attainment.

There are guidance materials available to help you assess children's work (DATA, 1995b) and it is an area of current research (Tufnell, 2000). Two key areas for development are:

- ensure that children have not just demonstrated a veneer of understanding;
- ensure that the work undertaken by the children is progressively more demanding. This is best done by assessing and analysing samples of children's designs and manufacture.

To do this aspect effectively you will need to record the way in which the child works as well as the final products that they make. Video recordings of discussion work and photographic evidence of final products helps here. If possible use digital recordings as these then allow the children to use them in project folders/booklets and make pertinent ICT links. It also means that you can instantly 'show and share' results rather than waiting for photographs to be developed (and know that they are in focus).

Getting the child to monitor and assess their own progress also helps them to increase their understanding and ownership of their learning. This could start with simple observations and recording of their own work going on (see below) to fully extended evaluations and analysis.

Figure 8. Recording requirements to make the car

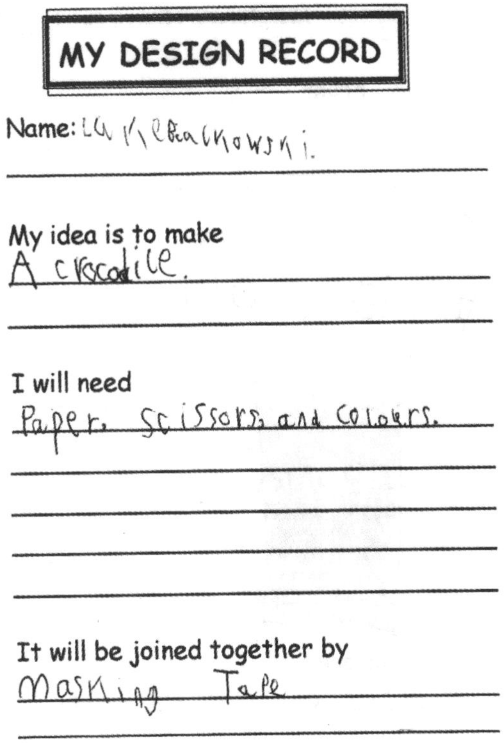

MY DESIGN RECORD

Name: Lu Krebackowski.

My idea is to make
A crocodile.

I will need
Paper, Scissors and Colours.

It will be joined together by
Masking Tape

Figure 9. Recording ideas, designs and evaluation for puppets (Year 2)
— from work provided by Liz Maclean

My chosen character is   A   ~~efati~~ crocodice.

Front   Back

Features are
Sharp teeth. Spikey back, large tongue and wide eyes.

Figure 10. Recording ideas, designs and evaluation for puppets (Year 2)
— from work provided by Liz Maclean

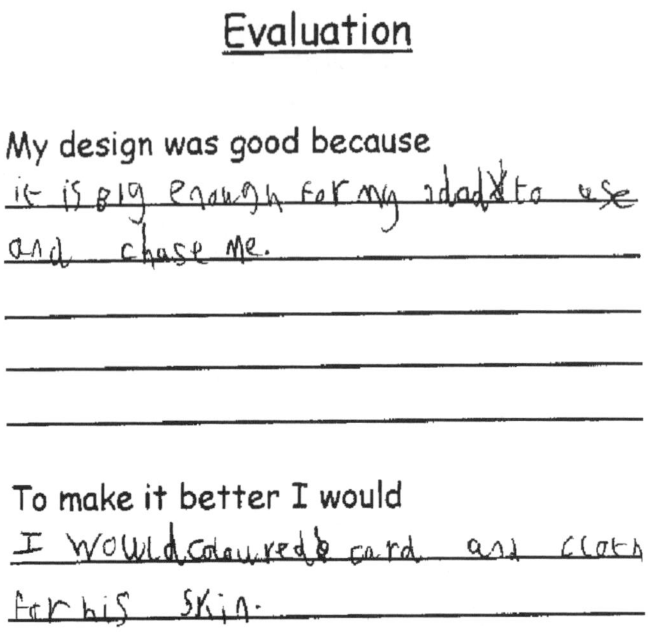

Evaluation

My design was good because

it is big enough for my 1dad(t to use and chase me.

To make it better I would

I would coloured card and cloth for his skin.

Figure 11. Recording ideas, designs and evaluation for puppets (Year 2)
– from work provided by Liz Maclean

Class management

The thoughts of teaching D&T (as with other practical activities) raise nightmare scenarios in the active imagination. Visions of children sticking themselves permanently to table tops, slicing fingers with scissors and knives, sawing desks and other mishaps flood our mind's eye before we can stop them. Not only do we have our fears to contend with but also those of other staff, the children and their parents! Any D&T activity can be safely conducted in the primary classroom provided that you have assessed all the possible risks and ensured as far as possible that they cannot happen.

The National Curriculum identifies key considerations for health and safety in D&T sessions. These conclude that when engaged in practical activities, particularly when using tools, equipment and materials, then the children need to be taught:

- **about hazards, risks and risk control;**
- **to recognise hazards, assess consequent risks and take steps to control the risks to themselves and others;**
- **to use information to assess the immediate and cumulative risks;**
- **to manage their environment to ensure the health and safety of themselves and others;**
- **to explain the steps they take to control risks.**

As the teacher you will need to provide risk assessments for practical activities that you plan to undertake. DATA's Research Paper 10 on health and safety (1995b), *Make It Safe* (NAAIDT, 1992) and *Be Safe!* (Abbott, 1990) provide model risk assessments for primary D&T activities. You will need to check with the school and local authority for their own guidelines too.

As previously stated it is important that the children take an active role in their own and others' health and safety. Please do not let your own fears restrict the availability of materials and equipment to your classes. If you are worried get more helpers or talk over your fears with more experienced staff for key tips and advice. Never be too proud to ask for advice, suggestions or reassurance. We all started at the beginning at some time and you will no doubt be able to reciprocate in other ways.

A fundamental part of the class management of D&T activities is the way that the teacher integrates the activities. When considering the management of your classroom you must consider the way in which you will deliver the activity.

WHY USE A SPIRAL CURRICULUM?

For effective learning to take place the learner needs to be exposed to similar but increasingly complex or different activities. We do not learn our alphabet the first time we hear it nor do we understand about number patterns without repetition, practice and increased intricacy that then develops our knowledge and understanding, developing intrinsic refinements through consolidation of learning.

D&T is best organised in a spiral manner so that the child continually builds upon what they have already learned (scaffolding). Thus, you need to continually revisit the curriculum, increasing what the children know and understand by consolidation and challenge.

WHAT IS THE ADVANTAGE OF USING GUIDED DISCOVERY LEARNING?

Discovery learning implies that knowledge is gained by and for oneself and the guidance implies that the discovery is not new to the guide. The children engage in activities that require them to search, manipulate, explore and investigate by themselves, in pairs or groups; but guided by the teacher. Very few discoveries happen by serendipity and even when they do, it takes the focused mind to notice them and the possible application. Children require careful background preparation in order for them to make discoveries.

Classroom example

Learning becomes more meaningful when we are allowed to actively explore our learning environment rather than listen passively to a teacher. Guided discovery helps children learn more effectively and, more importantly, it assists the development of life-long learning skills and thus the ability to know how to learn. For example if you want children in your class to be able to classify materials into different groups (e.g. wood, plastic, metal) as part of an FPT, rather than providing children with the basic material groups and examples for each, you could ask the children to provide the names of types of materials and examples of where they might be used. Then the children and you together could classify the materials by examining their similarities and differences. This approach is guided by the teacher to ensure that the classifications are correct, but the children are active contributors as they discover the similarities and differences between materials. This proactive approach reduces time 'off-task' and ensures that children feel that they are part of their learning and that the part they play is valued by the teacher and the rest of the class.

OUT-OF-SCHOOL WORK

As identified by the DfES through its QCA scheme of work, D&T provides valuable opportunities for work that can be conducted outside the classroom.

- *Product evaluation*: children could be given a framework to use as they evaluate a product, (e.g. a toy, a pop-up book, a piece of kitchen equipment or a bag);
- *Investigation of a mechanism*: children could be asked to find a particular mechanism (e.g. a lever, to list where it is found, how it works and to draw and label it);
- *Survey to discover people's preferences*: children could be asked to complete a survey to find out such information as a favourite sandwich or fabric;
- *Design drawings or prototypes*: children could be asked to draw some of their design ideas or to make a prototype of one of them (e.g. a card pop-up, a musical instrument);
- *Research*: children could carry out further research into a particular product (e.g. talking to family and friends, visiting the library, looking at artefacts in a shop, using books, magazines, CD-Roms, and the internet);
- *Carrying out practical activities*: children could practise skills under supervision (e.g. helping with food preparation, washing clothes as part of identifying systems and needs).

(Taken from Design and Technology – The National Curriculum for England, 1999 where other examples are given.)

INCLUSION

All children have the right to a good education and access to all areas of the curriculum. This means full participation in D&T activities and it is your duty as a teacher to see that this happens. If children in your class are not able to fully participate in a D&T activity then the activity needs to be either adapted or changed. QCA have identified the following potential barriers to learning in design and technology.

To overcome any, some children may require:

- alternative tasks to overcome any difficulties arising from specific religious beliefs they may hold in relation to the ideas or experiences they are expected to represent;
- alternative or adapted activities to overcome difficulties with manipulating tools, equipment or materials (for example, the use of computer-aided design and manufacture [CAD/CAM] to produce quality products, or the assistance of others to carry out activities according to the instructions of the child);
- specific support to enable them to engage in certain practical activities (for example, technological aids such as talking weighing scales, jigs to aid cutting,

kettle tipping devices, or specialist ICT software to help with sequencing and following instructions);

- opportunities to communicate through means other than writing or drawing and help to record or translate their design ideas into a drawing;
- opportunities to work in ways that avoid contact with materials to which they may be allergic;
- time and opportunity to use non-visual means to gain understanding about, and to evaluate, different products and to use this information to generate ideas;
- more time than others to complete the range of work indicated in breadth of study (for example, by doing shorter assignments, by combining experience in more than one material in an assignment).

In assessment:

- children who are unable to use tools will be unable to achieve certain aspects of the attainment target. When a judgement against level descriptions is required, assessment of progress should either discount aspects that relate to the use of tools or indicate the levels of support that were necessary to complete this work.

(Taken from Design and Technology – The National Curriculum for England, 1999.)

You need to note that are also specific references to design and technology in the examples for B/3a, B/3c, C/5b and C/5c.

Teaching design and technology :

a summary of key points

How can we improve standards in our teaching of design and technology?

— *Make an honest and analytical assessment of what you currently know, understand and can do in terms of design and technology (Ritchie, 1995).*

— *Continue to build upon this personal profile of professional development through in-service training (Ive, 1999).*

— *Share ideas and pool knowledge with other people.*

— *Ensure that the work undertaken by the children is progressively more demanding. This is best done by assessing and analysing samples of children's designs and manufacture.*

— *Ensure that the children have an adequate range of (and opportunity to deploy) materials and tools when designing and making.*

— *Ensure that children have not just demonstrated a veneer of understanding.*

Further reading

Bold, C. (1999) *Progression in Primary Design and Technology*. London: David Fulton. Accessible step-by-step approach to progression, what it is and how to do it. Includes photocopiable activity sheets.

Catlin, D. (1996) *Inventa Book of Mechanisms*. London: Valiant Technology. An idiot's guide to mechanisms. Clear explanations that show the maths too with diagrams appropriate to primary level.

Johnsey, R. (1998) *Exploring Primary Design and Technology*. London: Cassells. Explains how to do D&T.

Pathak, H. (1998) *Structural Package Designs*. The Netherlands: Pepin Press. Detailed plans of every box package design that you could think of.

Ritchie, R. (2001) *Primary Design and Technology: A Process for Learning*. (2nd edition) London: David Fulton. An excellent general book providing evidence of children's work and case studies.

Siraj-Blatchford, J. and MacLeod-Brudendell, I. (1999) *Supporting Science, Design and Technology in the Early Years*. Buckingham: Open University Press. Addressing D&T from an Early Years viewpoint. Activities related to socio-constructivist learning theories.

Journals

The Journal of Design and Technology Education
International Journal of Technology and Design Education

Useful websites

British Nutrition Foundation at www.nutrition.org.uk Provides impartial scientifically based nutritional knowledge and advice.

Crafts Council at www.craftscouncil.org.uk Promotes the contemporary crafts in Great Britain. It is an independent organisation funded by the Arts Council of England.

D&T Online at www.dtonline.org Offers free access to a wide range of D&T materials.

Design Museum at www.designmuseum.org This is the UK's biggest provider of design education resources and acts as a bridge between the design community, industry and education.

Design Council at www.design-council.org.uk Aims to improve the use of design on a personal and commercial level.

LEGO at www.lego.com Online projects for building with Lego and interactive experiences related to D&T control work.

Nuffield Curriculum Projects at www.Nuffield.org.primarydandt Support materials for D&T in schools. Online packs available for complete schemes of work and projects.

Science Museum at www.nmsi.ac.uk/welcome.html Provides interactive exhibits for D&T and science links.

Resources

ASE (Association for Science Education), College Lane, Hatfield, Hertfordshire AL10 9AA. Tel: 01707 267 411.

CRIPT (Centre for Research in Primary Technology), Faculty of Education - Attwood Building, University of Central England Birmingham, Franchise Street, Perry Barr, Birmingham B42 2SU. E-mail: cript@uce.ac.uk

DATA (Design and Technology Association), 16 Wellesbourne House, Walton Road, Wellesbourne, Warwickshire CV35 9JB. Tel: 01789 470007. Fax: 01789 841955. e-mail: data@data.org.uk www.data.org.uk This is the recognised professional association that represents all those involved in D&T education and as such is the bedrock support organisation for D&T teaching. Among many other useful and pertinent documents they have DfES supported packs to help teaching, technical vocabulary lists for each key stage and health and safety guidance. There is an annual DATA conference where the latest ideas are explored. DATA are also responsible for the *Journal of Design and Technology* which is published three times a year. Student membership is free.

NAAIDT (The National Association of Advisers and Inspectors in Design and Technology), 124 Kidmorw Road, Caversham, Reading RG4 7NB. Tel: 01734 470 615. www.naaidt.org.uk

The British Food Foundation, 52-54 High Holborn, London WC1V 6RQ. Tel: 0207 404 6505.

4 TEACHING PHYSICAL EDUCATION IN PRIMARY SCHOOLS

 ## The importance of PE
(adapted from QCA rationale for inclusion in the National Curriculum, 1999)

Physical education develops pupils' physical competence and confidence, and their ability to use these to perform in a range of activities.

- *It promotes physical skilfulness, physical development and a knowledge of the body in action.*
- *Physical education provides opportunities for pupils to be creative, competitive and to face up to different challenges as individuals and in groups and teams.*
- *It promotes positive attitudes towards active and healthy lifestyles.*

Pupils:

- *learn to think in different ways to suit a wide variety of creative, competitive and challenging activities;*
- *learn how to plan, perform and evaluate actions, ideas and performances to improve their quality and effectiveness.*

Through this process pupils discover their aptitudes, abilities and preferences, and make choices about how to get involved in lifelong physical activity.

A starting point

In the school context, PE is part of the educational process. In its wider sense it also introduces children to the rich cultural heritage of sport, exercise and dance in our society. In the pursuit of ensuring both the movement vocabulary and an entitlement to participation in its activities for all, PE facilitates regular opportunities for all-round learning experiences within the physical dimension.

Practical task

Learning objective: to consider what you bring to PE.

Identify your own starting point for teaching PE to primary-aged children. Do you bring any particular performance skills of your own to the area? Can you rationalise the importance of why teaching a child to become 'physically educated' is part of the whole education of the child, not something separate?

Personal values

Scene setting

If you are familiar with Thomas Hughes' *Tom Brown's Schooldays* (which is based on Dr Thomas Arnold's model of schooling at Rugby in the mid-nineteenth century) and claims that the Battle of Waterloo was won on the playing fields of Eton, then you will already appreciate how far PE has come since such days.

It was only the repercussions of the disastrous Second Boer War that signalled an appreciation that the physical condition of the populace was at a seriously low ebb. 'Drill' became a part of school provision for the masses from this period, moving through a number of European influences (for example, Swedish and German gymnastics) between the world wars, to a period when the term 'physical education' meant a multitude of different things to different people, very much dictated by personal experience.

Today PE has attained a status as one of the foundation subjects of the National Curriculum. It is a subject that can be studied to A level and to degree level within courses that lead to Qualified Teacher Status. In the primary school setting, the subject has a unique role in prioritising learning about the body and its movement potential. It is first and foremost a practical subject that seeks to provide opportunities for children to be physically active – supportive as that is to growing and developing young bodies.

Do you have to be physically gifted to teach PE?

The basic movement skills have been acquired by all of us by the time we enter our teens. By this time we have learnt a range of locomotor skills (like walking, running, jumping, skipping, hopping, etc) that will enable us to move competently in space and restricted areas. Additionally, the mastery of body balance (or stability), so crucial in supporting movement skills generally, will have enabled increasingly more challenging movement tasks to be successfully undertaken. Manipulative skills (for example catching and throwing, kicking a ball, striking a ball with a racket) will have become more refined and added to beyond the necessary fine motor skills of learning to write, use of a keyboard, and manipulation of a paint brush. These are all skills that as mature adults we should feel confident in performing ourselves, and though there is a recognition that we all have individual talents and weaknesses, just like in D&T or music or art, it is not beyond the capability of any teacher to teach PE effectively.

To substantiate this it is useful to be fully informed and aware of the key role the subject plays in the all-round development of children during the primary phase of learning. Primary teachers require a knowledge base about the subject in order to develop their own confidence in teaching the subject effectively to meet these needs. This process takes time, and can be nurtured through an appreciation of the subject's worth and its natural appeal to children. If there is also an enthusiasm, interest and vitality in play when confronted with the demands of teaching the subject's content, then it is highly likely that there will be benefits for all engaged in this particular teaching and learning context.

Practical task

Learning objective: to recall your own physical education.

What recall do you have of your own experiences in primary school PE? Do you remember apparatus work, country dancing, first attempts to throw bean bags accurately? Do you remember your school sports days, attempts to run in a lane for the first time, to jump into a sand pit? Do you remember learning to swim, or that first time away from home staying with your classmates (and your teachers!) in a centre designed for the purpose of learning in the great outdoors? Can you remember how you were taught? Do you recall experimentation with your own movement in gymnastic and dance activities, exploration of the properties and behaviours of a range of games equipment, practice and opportunity to surface your physical skills? Can you remember the particular strategies that teachers used when teaching you PE? Were they different from when you were taught other subjects?

Jot down your own recollections before reading on.

Here are some of the thoughts that a group of trainee teachers remembered about their primary school PE lessons.

- **'Country dancing ... first time I got to hold a girl's hand!'**
- **'Hoops, bean bags, quoits, skipping-ropes finding out what we could do with them.'**
- **'Lots of games of rounders ... not a lot of hitting, many 'no-balls', very poor fielding!'**
- **'Climbing on the big apparatus and learning to overcome my fear of heights.'**
- **'Best memories ... that field trip we went on where we did canoeing and abseiling and lots of other activities in the mud, the rain and the sunshine!'**
- **'Sports days ... running on a marked track, relays, long-jump, high-jump, throwing rounders and cricket balls for distance and measuring them at 40 and 50 metres plus.'**

Is PE in the primary school setting different today?

The places and venues in which the subject is taught remain the same (multi-purpose school halls, playgrounds, if fortunate grass fields and swimming pools, and possibly even purpose-built gymnasia or sports halls). The equipment used looks similar, even if it is now predominantly plastic and more colourful. There may even be more of it and variations of shape, texture and colour will be a notable feature of provision. The fact that there is now a status attached to the subject that did not previously exist is the major difference from pre-1992. That difference is that PE, like all other subjects in the curriculum, is a National Curriculum entitlement for all children and as such has to be taught throughout the age phases. This therefore means that teachers are required to have adequate subject knowledge to teach the subject and its areas of activity to a level that meets with the attainment targets and level descriptors for the Key Stages.

For teachers of the subject it is therefore necessary to acknowledge that physical education can claim some elements of 'uniqueness' when compared with other subject areas in the curriculum. It is the *only* subject that contributes to the education of the *whole child* (physical, cognitive and affective domains) through its main focus on the body and its movement potential. What is meant by this is that the central thrust of learning in PE is centred on building knowledge about how children's bodies move and which particular parts of those bodies are used to effect movement response to the particular tasks and activities typical of PE curricula. This developing understanding leads to enhanced motor control and skill acquisition, primary goals of an effective PE programme. As teachers we want children to *learn to move* and to *learn through movement*.

Furthermore, because it finds itself 'being learnt' in a variety of differing school locations and environments dependent on the activity being pursued (unlike other subjects that have a similar classroom-based home where learning takes place), PE is taught in school halls, sometimes in purpose-built gymnasia, on playgrounds, sometimes (luckily!) on playing fields, in sports halls and in swimming pools, and even at residential centres away from one's own school community. One's perspective of what PE 'looks like' is shaped by these features and often leads to an individual approach very much dictated by the context and environment associated with where we are required to teach the subject.

Another significant feature to note here is the way in which children *learn* PE. In the primary school setting there is a need to acknowledge that a great deal of children's physical development and skill learning lies before them. Physical education contributes markedly in this respect, and to the overall education of young people, by providing a setting for children to widen their functional and expressive range of movement potential and improve motor competence. Furthermore, PE gives the opportunity to reinforce conceptual understanding arising from other areas of the curriculum. In this respect it is similar to other areas of the curriculum in that its learning content is based around distinct skills, understanding and knowledge, as well as the very marked contributions (sometimes missed) it makes to key areas of learning, for example to literacy, numeracy and scientific components. Of further note should be an awareness that children participate in a wide range of physical pursuits outside of the school setting that clearly impact on their capacity to learn in those activities presented within the confines of the timetabled school week.

In their PE children are expected to make progress in their knowledge of the subject, the skills involved in participating in the subject areas of activity – dance, games, gymnastics, athletics, swimming, and outdoor and adventurous activities – and in their understanding of what participating in the subjects activities requires. This entails:

- *acquiring and developing skills;*
- *selecting and applying skills, tactics and compositional ideas;*
- *evaluating and improving performance;*
- *knowledge and understanding of fitness and health.*

Additionally, like all subject areas, PE's unique characteristics can also be utilised to instruct and motivate children across the spread of the curriculum in areas such as PSHE (Personal, Social and Health Education), SEN (Special Educational Needs), EAL (English as an Additional Language), citizenship, etc.

A good starting point for those seeking insight into the subject's rationale and basic philosophy might be to separate what 'PE' looks like in primary schools as distinct from notions of sport in schools. Issues that include recreational needs of children and common misconceptions that look upon the subject as an opportunity to 'let off steam', which all children in the age phase undoubtedly need, also require consideration.

PE in the primary school needs to serve a variety of different purposes. Foremost amongst these should be the importance of teaching children about the needs of regular and healthy exercise, the understanding required to identify how important our body is to an active lifestyle, and a respect for the fact that with regular exposure to a breadth and variety of activities, children become increasingly skilled, competent and confident in what their bodies can do.

Rationalising the subject can help in developing this understanding. Through *purposeful activity* physical education can provide the following:

- **development of physical competence and the promotion of physical development;**
- **opportunities to experience the benefits of physical participation which can be developed in adult life;**
- **opportunities for appreciation of both skilful and creative performances within varied areas of activity.**

When taught effectively physical education can contribute to:

- **developing problem-solving skills;**
- **increasing confidence and self-esteem;**
- **the development of inter-personal skills.**

In essence the activity focus of physical education should combine 'the thinking involved in making decisions and selecting, refining, judging and adapting movements' (*PE and the National Curriculum, 1992*). Through an immersion in the range of activities that a well balanced physical education programme offers, children should be 'encouraged to develop the personal qualities of commitment, fairness and enthusiasm' (*ibid*), and learn how to think in different ways to suit the variety of activities.

> 'They learn how to plan, perform and evaluate actions, ideas and performances to improve the quality of their effectiveness. Through this process children discover their aptitudes, abilities and preferences, and make choices about how to get involved in lifelong physical activity' (*PE and the National Curriculum*, 1999).

It is therefore crucial that teachers of the subject understand that there is an inter-related process for learning in PE covering planning, performing and evaluating. Similarly, for each strand in this process there are at least two elements of progression, namely difficulty and quality. How and to what extent each element is developed will depend on the age, ability and previous experience of the children. Knowledge and experience of the process of teaching and learning in PE is acquired by teachers over time, through an immersion in the subject content to assist planning needs, and through its delivery to children.

Teachers therefore need to:

- **organise the teaching setting – the space available for the PE lesson, and the safety considerations involved in this;**
- **anticipate the resources needed to support the learning including time constraints;**
- **provide and deliver skill learning opportunities;**
- **pitch lesson content at a level related to children's existing skill, knowledge and understanding;**
- **build on previous learning.**

Physical education at its best level of provision might seek 'to set aside a portion of every school day for large-muscle activities that encourage and develop *learning to move* and *learning through movement*' (Gallahue, 1998).

- **The learning-to-move aim of PE is based on acquiring movement skills and enhancing physical fitness.**
- **The learning-through-movement aim of PE is based on the fact that effective PE can positively affect both the cognitive and affective (social/emotional) development of children.**

Knowledge about child development and growth equips those charged with the responsibility of teaching children with a firm basis for knowing when children are ready to be introduced to concepts and skills.

Practical task

Learning objective: to decide which growth and development characteristics you need to consider when planning for children's PE.

Look at the following child growth and development characteristics. Make a checklist for yourself to supplement how these statements would impact on PE provision in your own school placement. Consider particularly time constraints for younger and older children in the light of these parameters.

Child growth and development

At 5 years, children:
- **are usually self-confident and show off;**
- **are able to be generous and friendly;**
- **love to learn new things;**
- **have good control of emotions;**
- **can be persistent in learning a new skill;**
- **ask lots of questions;**
- **can play alone for long periods but also like to play with others;**
- **love stories and have lively, busy minds;**
- **need lots of encouragement and approval for achievements from adults.**

At 6 years, children:
- **tend to be irritable and rebellious but can also be friendly and helpful;**
- **are very curious;**
- **find failure difficult;**
- **begin to read and need some help from adults;**
- **may have a particular friend;**
- **need lots of rest and sleep.**

At 7 years, children:
- **are very active and energetic; more stable than at age 6;**
- **find it difficult to control their own energy;**
- **enjoy reading and watching television;**
- **are less dependent on adults;**
- **need lots of rest and sleep.**

Between 8 and 11 years, children:
- **are well co-ordinated in terms of physical activity;**
- **are emotionally independent of adults;**
- **are able to control emotions to a large extent;**
- **need adults to give firm boundaries;**
- **are argumentative;**
- **know good from bad and true from false;**
- **size up adults;**
- **feel it is important to be believed;**
- **are sexually curious, but in thought rather than in deed;**
- **are very perceptive;**
- **listen to adults and are trustful in matters they consider important.**

From: NSPCC and The National Coaching Foundation (1995) *Protecting Children – A Guide for Sportspeople*. Leeds: The National Coaching Foundation.

SOME THOUGHTS ABOUT TIME ALLOCATIONS FOR THE SUBJECT

There is clearly the need to allocate reasonable periods of time for PE provision in the primary school timetable. The fact that it is a 'crowded' curriculum should not override the importance of adequate time being set aside for the physical needs of children. Indeed, if we look at early years provision we see that there is a great emphasis on play, outdoor provision and activities that focus on developing locomotor, stability and manipulative skills. These types of activities happen every day in nursery and reception settings.

What is clear is that appropriate amounts of time need to be set aside each week for PE activity. How much time is influenced by the age and developmental needs of the children, so for infants that may well be several periods of the week, whereas with juniors longer, more concentrated time allocations are needed. The overriding concern should be recognising the importance of such provision for growing bodies, and quality PE experiences that are conducive to servicing these needs. It is not a matter of piece-meal *ad hoc* provision, much more a case of planned, regular, consistently delivered PE. If two 45-minute periods a week were regarded as a minimum at Key Stage 2, and this was maintained throughout the year, then the benefits would be marked. If this had built on similar, say two 30-minute sessions a week during Key Stage I, then the overall picture would be greater consistency in children's performance levels in the subject area, and significantly contribute to the status of PE in both teachers' and children's eyes.

All of this of course is part of overall curriculum planning and clear school policy on such matters. An awareness of how much PE could be covered across the whole period of a child's time in primary school would lend insight to such decision-making. Starting from a basic premise of two periods a week of PE from Year I through to Year 6 (assuming a 39-week year), then 78 possible lessons a year to a total of 468 across the six years is the kind of provision to secure in depth what needs to be covered for children aged 5 to II to become 'physically educated'.

In PE children are required to:

- **acquire a range of basic movement skills;**
- **accumulate knowledge and understanding of their own and others' movement;**
- **apply this skill and understanding when they:**
  - **plan physical activities**
  - **participate in physical activities**
  - **evaluate physical activities.**

Basic movement skills

Basic movement skills include:

Gymnastics	Dance	Games
Run	Jump	Send
Jump	Twist / Turn	Receive
Roll	Gesture	Strike
Vault	Balance	Rebound
Climb	Bend	Travel with
Balance	Stretch	Dispossess

How do children acquire motor skills?

A basic analysis of what PE is composed of could (also) begin by looking at three common themes. The importance of children mastering stability, locomotion and manipulative skills is crucial to learning in PE, and not just in its core activities of games, dance and gymnastics, but also to life generally. It is not difficult to demonstrate the crucial association of these elements as early as the beginnings of challenging a child to run with a ball in their hands across a set distance to turn and return to where they started – without a basic mastery of locomotive skills, balance and grip the task cannot be met. Other activities will draw from further refinement and a greater demand on specific elements, such as a child performing a complex balance like a headstand. The point here is to recognise that children require continuity in the work being covered, challenge within tasks set, and further practice and consolidation of previously learnt skills and techniques so that they can advance their learning and knowledge in the field.

All teachers need to recognise that children have different potential and different physical, emotional and intellectual characteristics, and though they may be of the same chronological age their developmental age can often vary by as much as three years. This means that they will learn skills at different rates. We need to recognise therefore that children acquire motor skills through a process that looks like this:

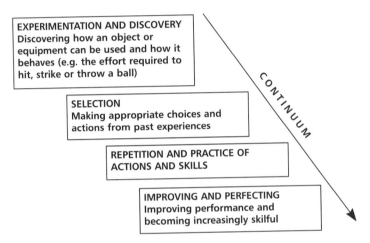

Knowledge and understanding

In order that teachers can *teach* effective PE in primary school settings they need to:

- **know about PE in the curriculum – about the subject, its aims and learning intentions;**
- **possess knowledge and understanding about the subject's activity areas, specifically dance, gymnastics and games (and increasingly, as children develop their aptitudes and skills, also about swimming, athletics, and outdoor and adventurous activities);**
- **understand the principles and practice regarding teaching methodology (with particular reference to planning, teaching and class management);**
- **be aware of safety aspects within their planning and preparation of lesson content;**
- **be able to observe, evaluate and assess children's performances against relevant criteria;**
- **set up a monitoring/assessment record-keeping system to enable reporting and accountability for their teaching of the subject;**
- **keep abreast of National Curriculum considerations and on-going developments and issues within the subject area;**
- **identify and look for opportunities to develop cross-curricular links and learning with other subjects through their teaching of PE.**

The impact of such learning should therefore lead to the following:

- **a raised awareness of the key role that PE plays in the all-round development of children in the primary phase of learning (Early Years, Key Stage 1, Key Stage 2 specifically);**
- **a developed and working knowledge base related to how the subject meets children's specific needs (this will include effective methods of teaching and learning);**
- **a knowledge of ways in which appropriate lesson plans and units of work may be prepared, with particular reference to the NC Programmes of Study;**
- **a knowledge of safety aspects in the teaching of the subject and the position of the teacher in relation to the law;**
- **a knowledge of a wide range of resources and materials to assist with planning, teaching and assessment of teaching the subject in primary schools.**

In order to meet the requirements contained within the four cells of the ITT (Initial Teacher Training) curriculum (Knowledge and Understanding; Planning, Teaching and Class Management; Monitoring, Assessment, Recording, Reporting and Accountability; Other Professional Requirements) teachers of the subject need to know about:

- **physical, psychomotor, cognitive and affective aspects of child development linked to experiences in PE;**
- **appropriate general and specific movement skills, and the underpinning biomechanical and physiological principles, as they particularly apply to NC Programmes of Study;**
- **the role of the teacher and approaches to the teaching of PE, including teaching and learning styles;**
- **lesson content, structure and organisation and the importance of 'units' of work to maintain continuity and progression;**
- **observation, evaluation, assessment and recording and reporting strategies;**
- **safety aspects and the responsibilities of the teacher in teaching PE;**
- **resources, resource issues, and the utilisation of such in teaching delivery;**
- **award schemes – appropriateness, relevance, usefulness and suitability;**
- **establishing the notion of 'inclusion', equality of opportunity, and issues of gender, ethnicity, class and special needs;**
- **potential for cross-curricular links where appropriate and relevant;**
- **the specific language associated with the subject and how this builds on that learnt elsewhere.**

Health and safety

Physical education is a subject with readily identifiable health and safety considerations. By their very nature the activities that form the content of the PE curriculum have elements of challenge and thereby risk attached to them. In reality, this is why there exists a tendency for teachers to be over cautious or even anxious about issues of too much equipment, allowing too much freedom in the space that is used for PE activity, and wary of children over-extending themselves when it comes to scaling heights or using the apparatus associated with gymnastic activities.

Take the risk element away from the activities however and the challenge to learning and performance levels also becomes diluted. There is no allowance, nor compromise to be made when considering children's health and safety in school settings.

The Health and Safety at Work Act, 1974, describes the responsibilities of employers to people who work for them. Within these responsibilities, there is a duty to ensure that:

> '… persons not in … employment who may be affected are not exposed to risks to their health or safety.'

In other words it is the school that has the responsibility not to expose its children to any unacceptable risks regarding personal health and safety.

There are various safety codes in existence for PE mostly based on good practice. Teachers have to be aware of dangers and risks and need to take steps to deal with them. This idea is part of the 'parental' responsibility role that teachers have. Schools and teachers have to make sure that:

- surfaces, equipment and buildings are safe;
- procedures for safety, first aid and emergencies are in place;
- children are warned of the risks and discouraged from inappropriate behaviour;
- children are prepared properly for the activity;
- the activity follows approved and appropriate guidelines and that they take all necessary safety measures;
- parental consent is obtained for trips, outdoor and adventurous activities, etc.

Teachers need to know about anything that might affect children taking part in physical activities, including personal fears, asthma, disabilities, diabetes, heart problems, epilepsy, etc and they need to treat that information confidentially, with understanding of the potential embarrassment for the person involved.

First aid boxes should be available, properly equipped with contents that are regularly checked to maintain provision levels. Teachers are also encouraged to know first aid procedures and to have a first aid qualification.

Safety requirements for specific activities are available from National Governing Bodies and associations. Some activities, including outdoor pursuits and swimming, require a specific qualification to be held by the teacher, in addition to a recognised teaching certificate or degree.

Practical task

Learning objective: to appreciate why health and safety factors figure so highly in planning for PE.

Describe the safety measures you have observed teachers taking when providing and delivering PE lessons. Note how children's behaviour is intrinsically involved in the notion of safe practice.

It is an important element of learning in PE that children develop a sense of personal responsibility for their own health and safety. Teachers and children working together make situations as safe as possible and children's behaviour influences the standards of health and safety that are in place in any particular teaching session. It is a good idea to engage children's thinking in this by posing them the following set of questions in order to maximise confidence levels for all parties:

1. Could you behave in a safer way?
2. What should you do with personal items of jewellery, watches etc?
3. Do you know the correct ways of supporting people in some activities, e.g. gymnastics?
4. Do you know how to handle, get out, put away equipment safely?
5. Do you get carried away sometimes, and lose self control?
6. Do you wear the correct clothing and safety equipment for the activity, e.g. shin guards, hand guards, gum shields etc?
7. Do you know where the first aid boxes are?
8. Are you properly prepared to take part in the activity? Do you know what to do and how to do it?
9. Do you follow your teacher's instructions?
10. Do you warm up and cool down properly?

There are many things that children can do to make PE safe and fun. Children do rely on the teacher's guidance and support but need to play their part too. Being safe in PE involves a partnership between teacher and children and children with other children. This is an on-going requirement of well-taught PE lessons, where as part of the preliminaries before action and movement take place effective teaching involves highlighting particular priorities (and reminders) under the health and safety umbrella for the lesson that follows.

Safe lifting

Children can injure themselves if they do not learn to lift properly. Think about children carrying games equipment as well as the more obvious movement required for often heavy, awkward gymnastic apparatus. Bad habits formed at an early age can seriously affect later life health and active recreation. Teachers therefore need to ensure that children:

- **only lift weights and objects that are manageable;**
- **bend their knees (not their backs!), keep their backs straight, and use leg, hip and shoulder muscles to lift as they are normally stronger than the arms;**
- **carry the weight as close to the body as possible;**
- **keep their feet approximately shoulder-width apart.**

Such principles apply whether children are lifting on their own or in cooperation with others: send the message *'Always be careful!'*

Checklist

1. Children should not be exposed to health and safety risks.
2. Schools and teachers have a duty of care.
3. Specific safety guidelines are available for all PE activities.
4. Children have an increasing role to play in making PE safe.
5. Safe lifting is very important not least for developing lifelong good habits.

Children need to be aware of health and safety risks and work with them in mind so as to minimise their impact – and they also need to be made aware that they cannot be totally eliminated.

Practical task

Learning objective: to understand why 'risk assessment' is so crucial to planning for safe PE.

What follows is a basic check list for delivering 'safe' PE – carry out your own risk assessment of an observed or personally delivered lesson with the following in mind:

1. **Is the children's clothing suitable for the activity in which they are to participate?**
2. **Are the children barefooted for dance and gymnastics work?**
3. **Is the teacher suitably clothed to allow for movement themselves in the workspace?**
4. **Have the children removed jewellery and tied back long hair?**
5. **Is the floor surface clean and tidy?**
6. **Is there sufficient space for the range of activities to take place?**
7. **Can the teacher observe the whole class working at all times (within reason)?**
8. **Did the children engage in a warm-up and a cool-down activity?**
9. **Are clear start and stop signals given?**
10. **Are all abilities catered for in the course of the lesson?**
11. **Are resources used accessible, clean and stored appropriately?**
12. **Was the lesson well planned, controlled and disciplined?**
13. **Was first aid readily available and accessible?**

Could you add anything extra to this list having carried out the task in a 'real life' scenario?

Cross-curricular links

Physical education makes an important and significant contribution to the National Curriculum's aim of promoting learning 'across the curriculum'.

The promotion of spiritual, moral, social and cultural development, key skills and thinking skills can (and does!) happen through the teaching of PE as the examples below demonstrate.

Promoting children's spiritual, moral, social and cultural development through PE

PE provides opportunities to promote the following.

- *Spiritual development*, through helping children gain a sense of achievement and develop positive attitudes towards themselves (for example, scoring a goal for the first time, having a sense of pride in being a member of a team).
- *Moral development*, through helping children gain a sense of fair play based on rules and the conventions of activities, develop positive sporting behaviour, know how to conduct themselves in sporting competitions and accept authority and support referees, umpires and judges (for example, in playing games with rules to abide by, playing in a defined area, accepting decisions made within the game).
- *Social development*, through helping children develop social skills in activities involving cooperation and collaboration, responsibility, personal commitment, loyalty and teamwork, and considering the social importance of physical activity, sport and dance (for example, working with a partner or group to devise matching and mirroring sequences for gymnastics or dance activities).
- *Cultural development*, through helping children experience and understand the significance of activities from their own and other cultures (for example, folk dances and traditional games), recognise how activities and public performance gives a sense of cultural identity, and consider how sport can transcend cultural boundaries (for example learning games from different countries and cultures).

(Taken from *Physical Education – The National Curriculum for England*, 1999, where other examples are given.)

Promoting key skills through PE

PE provides opportunities for children to develop these key skills.

- *Communication*, through promoting verbal and non-verbal communication skills when explaining what they intend to do, giving feedback to others, planning and organising group or team work, giving instructions and signals in a game, using gesture in dance, and through responding to music and sounds in dance (for example, communicating verbally with a partner in recognising performance qualities in a gymnastic sequence).
- *Application of number*, through collecting and analysing data (for example, to find their scoring average in a game from shots taken), using different forms of measurement such as calculating the distance jumped against the percentage of their body height, understanding and using grid references and bearings in outdoor and adventurous activities, using a variety of measuring and recording equipment to take pulse, heart rates and temperatures, and using stopwatches and tapes to measure performance in running, jumping and throwing (in athletic activities).
- *IT*, through collecting, analysing and interpreting data to evaluate performance and identify priorities for improvement (for example, using video technology with digital tracking to analyse movement performance and technique, using spreadsheets to record and analyse results in athletic and swimming activities, and using databases to build their ideas, improve and record their performance).

vith others, through taking on a variety of roles in groups and teams in
e activities, working in a group with a collective goal and deciding on
o meet it, cooperating with others by observing rules and
s when competing against them (for example, in outdoor and
ous activities where teamwork challenges, problem-solving and
ial endeavour are high on the personal development agendas of all those
participating).

- *Improving own learning and performance*, through recognising what they do well
and what they need to do better, helping them to observe a good performance
and to imitate it, and develop the confidence to try something new (for
example, in constructing a gymnastic sequence using apparatus, and learning
from other children's demonstrations and how that can benefit individual
performance levels).
- *Problem solving*, through recognising the nature of the task or challenge, thinking
of different ways to approach the task and changing their approach as the need
arises, and understanding and applying the principles of movement strategy and
composition to the task (for example, in solving how to break down an
opposition's defence by organising your own team differently).

(Taken from *Physical Education – The National Curriculum for England*, 1999, where
other examples are given.)

Promoting other aspects of the curriculum

PE provides opportunities to promote other aspects.

- *Thinking skills*, through helping children to consider information and concepts
that suit the different activities and critically evaluate aspects of performance,
and to generate and express their own ideas and opinions about tactics, strategy
and composition (for example, movement response to a range of different
stimuli based around a theme of 'feelings' and the important role that language
plays within this).
- *Work-related learning*, through helping children to run and organise sports and
dance competitions and festivals, to take different roles including chair,
secretary, treasurer, to manage and book facilities in school for children to use,
and to assist teachers' work with younger children in a variety of exercise, sport
and dance clubs (for example, utilising the support of elder children in extra-
curricular settings to 'coach' younger children in basic skills performance).
- *Education for sustainable development*, through developing children's knowledge
and understanding of healthy lifestyles and of different, challenging
environments (for example, applying a range of physical skills in response to
changing weather conditions in a field-team game or on a geography field
course).

(Taken from *Physical Education – The National Curriculum for England*, 1999, where
other examples are given.)

Practical task

Learning objective: to consider what else PE provides beyond its emphasis on learning to move increasingly skilfully and competently.

Using the PoS (Programmes of Study) headings construct the beginnings of your own checklist to highlight the particular contributions that different PE areas make towards spiritual, moral, social, and cultural development, key skills and thinking skills and citizenship. Add to this as your own experience, knowledge and understanding of teaching PE develops.

Use of ICT

Physical Education – The National Curriculum for England (1999) states the following:

Use of information and communication technology across the curriculum.

1. Children should be given opportunities to apply and develop their ICT capability through the use of ICT tools to support their learning in all subjects (*with the exception of PE at Key Stages I and 2*).

2. Children should be given help to support their work by being taught to:

   a) find things out from a variety of sources, selecting and synthesising the information to meet their needs and developing an ability to question its accuracy, bias and plausibility;

   b) develop their ideas using ICT tools to amend and refine their work and enhance its quality and accuracy;

   c) exchange and share information, both directly and through electronic media;

   d) review, modify and evaluate their work, reflecting critically on it, as it progresses.

Despite what we read in statement I above, the subject of PE can benefit enormously from the support of ICT related resources. A number of examples where ICT can support teaching and learning in PE and be used by teachers and children follows:

- **use of digital cameras and videos to record (and follow up with analysis) performed work;**
- **use of CD-Rom to research activity being followed in PE lessons;**
- **use of video support (learning from the 'stars') to enhance skill development;**
- **monitoring and recording individual performance using spreadsheets and databases;**
- **producing task cards and prompt sheets to support learning in activity sessions;**
- **display purposes for PE notice-boards and skills charts.**

Without forgetting that the emphasis in PE needs to focus upon performance aspects, in other words the practical 'doing' of the subject, we need to recognise how ICT can augment, improve by information gathered and improve potential future performance. The skill lies in the teacher recognising when it is practical, relevant and purposeful to utilise such resources, without losing sight of the primary emphasis throughout their teaching of PE.

Teaching

How can we improve standards in our teaching of PE?

The key to successful teaching in PE is the promotion of an approach that is consistent with what is deemed to be 'good primary practice' – that is a child-focused, problem-solving model that ensures that all children will benefit from their experiences in the subject area. A yardstick to work by should be to have high expectations of children's performances in the subject area – after all children do participate in a great variety of out-of-school activity that has at its root physical performance. They bring this experience with them to school and it is in their PE lessons that their skills should be further challenged and developed by offering a range of different activity areas to utilise these skills.

It is also important to stress the need for an individual teacher's practice to be a part of a whole school policy towards teaching PE. This enables the effective implementation of the National Curriculum for the subject area, and identifies the key factors that determine how particular (individual) schools can deliver a programme that is varied in its content, yet also matches the specific conditions, facilities and resources available in those schools. This lends itself to a continuous and progressive approach across the age phase and promotes appropriate learning opportunities set within a context of child development and growth.

Practical task

Learning objective: to decide what information can be gathered before moving ahead with planning individual lessons in the subject.

Conduct a PE audit of your current school placement under the following headings:

- *facilities and resources;*
- *programmes of study taught;*
- *documentation in place;*
- *coordinator's role;*
- *assessment and record-keeping employed;*
- *INSET delivered and planned.*

Analyse shortfalls, and include a summative statement that pinpoints which areas need attention to improve PE provision in the school reviewed.

What are the characteristics of a good PE activity? The following represents the types of guidance that would support good practice and are suggested here as markers by which to judge well planned, taught and assessed PE lessons.

Physical education

Guidance for good practice

1. Lessons are pre-empted by a controlled changing session prior to entering the workspace.

   - Are children alerted to what they will be doing during the lesson to follow?
   - Are they asked to immediately set about an activity on entering the workspace?
   - Is the mood and tone of the lesson set even before the children enter the workspace?
   - Such detail should be noted in the lesson plan for the session.

2. A set format is followed in the delivery of the session.

   - Warm-up, skills practice, skills application, cool-down activity.
   - Are children engaged in the three strands of PE learning within the session – planning, performance, evaluation, with a key emphasis on the performance (the actual physical activity) element?
   - Are children challenged with the content?
   - Do they have opportunities to watch others, and are they invited to comment on such work?
   - Is a range of demonstration strategies applied within the session (individual children, pairs, groups, half class, teacher)?
   - Are issues relating to health and hygiene addressed within sessions?
   - Do children have opportunities to work individually, in pairs or in small groups?
   - Is there visible evidence to note progression in the work, building on prior knowledge and experience, leading to an improved quality of work?

3. The use of a wide variety of equipment and resources is available (and used) in sessions.

   - Do these support learning across the range of ability?
   - Is provision made for both ends of the spectrum of ability as well as the general majority?
   - Are allocated work areas clearly defined for children (boundaries marked, etc)?
   - Are the children aware of the potential usage of equipment?
   - Are they encouraged to make their own decisions on how best to use the equipment to enable a level of success to surface prior to technical input?
   - Are they instructed in working safely with due regard to others, and with regard to using equipment correctly?
   - Do they display an ability to take growing responsibility for their own and others' safety?

4. Lessons are satisfactorily concluded.

   - When appropriate a satisfactory (physical) cool-down activity is included.
   - There is a follow-up to work done during the session through verbal discussion and review of work covered.

- Highlighted areas to work on in future sessions are noted.
- The children are asked to comment on how things went, to identify aspects of their work they feel were improved, and those that need further practice.
- Were the children asked about how they felt about the session?
- Did they enjoy the activities?
- What specifically did they like/dislike about the session?
- What have the children learned from their lesson?

5. There is a discernible teaching style conducive to the nature of the subject.
   - Is variation in teaching style evident, including presentation and feedback skills?
   - One that conveys an enthusiasm and interest with the teaching material, and a willingness to participate alongside the children's learning.
   - There is also a variation in teaching strategies used that ensures maximum levels of participation and access to session content for all. These include open and closed skill practices, problem-solving activities, opportunities for individual creativity, as well as work that builds on individual, collaborative and team work, together with competitive challenges, either self-based or with/against others.

Practical task

Learning objective: to understand what to expect of children's performance levels in PE at key points in their primary schooling.

Watch the SCAA (1997) video 'Expectations in Physical Education at Key Stages 1 and 2', using the accompanying booklet. Make a set of personal notes on the performance levels observed and identify the features of performance that mark out different children observed across the different year groups (2, 4 and 6).

It is important to stress the need for the individual teacher's practice to be a part of a whole school policy towards teaching PE. This enables the effective implementation of the National Curriculum for the subject area, and identifies the key factors that determine how particular (individual) schools can deliver a programme that is varied in its content (the 'breadth of study' notion), yet also matches to the specific conditions, facilities and resources available in those schools. In addition, 'teaching should ensure that when evaluating and looking to improve performance, connections are made between developing, selecting and applying skills, tactics and compositional ideas, and fitness and health' (*Physical Education – The National Curriculum for England*, 1999).

The Programmes of Study in the National Curriculum for Physical Education provide the basis for planning work. They set out what children should be taught in the subject area and provide a basis for planning schemes or units of work. Schools need to also consider the general teaching requirements for inclusion, use of language, use of ICT, and health and safety that apply across the programmes of study when planning (see NCPE documentation).

Individual teachers may wish to draw exemplar material from the DfES/QCA schemes of work at Key Stages 1 and 2 that demonstrate how the programmes of study and the attainment targets for the subject can be translated into practical, manageable teaching plans. In Appendices A and B you will find two examples of units of work, one for Key Stage 1 games and the other for Key Stage 2 gymnastics, that illustrate this.

Practical task

Learning objective: to appreciate that learning from example and contextualising the setting will help planning in the medium term.

Choose an area of PE activity and a year group at which to aim the planning, and draw up your own example of a unit of work. Use the examples cited above to help you and the following checklist of issues to consider when setting about such a task.

Planning a unit of work

Consider the following:

- **children's ages and numbers involved;**
- **prior experience/range of ability;**
- **facility provision/equipment available;**
- **time allocation;**
- **National Curriculum Programmes of Study references;**
- **'whole curriculum' planning considerations;**
- **teaching approach/strategies and styles;**
- **information required for the children;**
- **assessment criteria;**
- **recording and reporting strategies.**

Teaching strategies

Consider the following guidance.

What standards of behaviour are expected when:

- **the children are getting changed?**
- **they enter the workspace (hall, playground, swimming-pool)?**
- **you give the signal to stop?**
- **you (or another child) is talking?**
- **they get the equipment out?**
- **you are talking and they have the equipment?**
- **they are selecting partners/groups?**
- **they want to gain your attention?**
- **they put the equipment away?**
- **they leave the lesson?**

PE knowledge and skills need to be taught and consolidated, but creating a positive learning environment in PE takes time and, as in the classroom, good working routines need to be taught – they don't just happen!

For the teaching of PE it is essential therefore to note the following.

- **Provide opportunities for children to measure and compare their own performances with others.**
- **Allow ample time to enable children to progress their skills performances through repetition, practice and application across a range of different activities.**
- **Planning in units (over approximately half-term periods) facilitates the above.**
- **Review and modify provision as a result of children's response and progress.**

Classroom example

There is a difference in teaching children in early years settings, at Key Stage 1 and Key Stage 2. It would be inappropriate to expect very young children to construct complex gymnastic sequences as much as it would be to anticipate 11 year-olds responding in dance to stimuli based around nursery rhymes. This tells us that setting tasks within the capabilities, interests and abilities of children is just as crucial to PE as other subjects. The teaching approach adopted needs to reflect this understanding of children's different needs as they move through the primary phase. The appreciation of how children learn skills, the changes children's bodies go through from 3 to 11, with children's readiness to learn are crucial to learning in PE. A teacher's style of delivery, their own knowledge base of the activity to be pursued, and their awareness of being able to break down learning into simple steps, or extend the work, are all influential in providing the best of experiences for the children in their PE lessons.

Monitoring and assessment

Children's attainment should be recorded at intervals throughout each key stage. At the Foundation Stage this should be completed and based on the physical development area of learning noted in the Curriculum Guidance for the Foundation Stage (2000) for children in this phase of their education. Such records should be used to help the planning of future work and to form the basis for reports made at the end of each stage of learning. They can also be used for interim reports, for example end of year written reports and to inform parents at meetings during the course of a year.

All activities provide opportunities for assessment. However, it will not always be appropriate to carry out full scale, across the whole class assessment in every PE lesson. More useful to the everyday practitioner is to develop/establish criteria that can be used in assessing children's work in PE. Examples of criteria that might characterise 'good performance' in PE are:

- **accuracy;**
- **efficiency;**

- **adaptability;**
- **ability to do more than one thing at a time;**
- **good line or design;**
- **sustaining participation;**
- **imaginative performance.**

Using the end of end of key stage level descriptors and attainment targets for PE helps to establish a basis for achievement.

> 'Each level description describes the types and range of performance that pupils working at that level should characteristically demonstrate the level descriptions provide the basis for making judgements about pupils' performance at the end of Key Stages 1, 2 and 3 in deciding on a pupils' level of attainment at the end of a key stage, teachers should judge which description best fits the pupils' performance. When doing so, each description should be considered alongside descriptions for adjacent levels' (*Physical Education – The National Curriculum for England*, 1999).

> Teachers also need to consider what methods exist to collect evidence of children's attainment. Direct observation is the most obvious form, particularly as physical performance is instantly recognised and is a feature of learning in the subject during the primary age phase. Other strategies to utilise are noted below, along with a criteria base for observing children 'doing PE activities'.

OBSERVATION
Watching children doing PE activities.

1. Is the class working safely? Consider:
   - care;
   - control;
   - response to task.

2. Is the class answering the task? Consider whether they are:
   - listening;
   - understanding;
   - responding appropriately;
   - being challenged?

3. How well is the task being answered?
   - are the skills/techniques being learned and applied?
   - are the ideas appropriate?
   - what is the quality of performance?

4. How can I help?
   - feedback/further guidance;
   - clarification;
   - teaching points;
   - demonstration;

- discussion;
- suggestion;
- praise/encouragement/criticism/reflection.

EVALUATION
- Observation.
- Interpretation.

Practical task

Learning objective: to practise your own skills and abilities in observation.

Observe a PE lesson and identify what particular assessment you want to carry out (it might focus on a particular skill or technique being practised). Contrast two individual children's performances and evaluate the outcomes, adding where the work needs to go next for each child. Justify your appraisals of performance and how you would provide consolidation and further development of skills performance if you were to take the follow-on lesson.

Possible assessment strategies

- Children's verbal response to the teacher's questioning.
- Children's physical/visual response to the teacher's questioning and task setting.
- Children's own questioning of peers and teachers.
- Teacher observation of the practical demonstration, verbal response, written answers from the children.
- Children's own review and analysis of performance.
- Children may work in an open skill situation.
- Video of the performance – child response and feedback.
- A third party provides performance feedback.
- Children's response to a task card, criteria or teacher verbal instructions.
- Child response to performance against identified criteria or teacher verbal instructions.

Children may gather evidence of their performance from several sources:

- external feedback;
- internal feeling – self-assessment;
- third party verbal response;
- photographic and/or video feedback.

For the teaching and assessment of PE it is essential to note the following.

- **Provide opportunities for children to measure and compare their own performances with others.**
- **Allow ample time to enable children to progress their skill performances through repetition, practice and application across a range of different activities.**

- Planning in units (over approximately half-term periods) facilitates the above.
- Review and modify provision as a result of children's response and progress.

WORK OUTSIDE THE CLASSROOM

Many units provide opportunities for teachers to set worthwhile tasks that can be completed outside formal teaching time. Suitable tasks include:

- practising specific skills;
- activities that promote health;
- watching live or recorded sport and dance;
- getting ideas and information using ICT.

Most schools offer a range of extra-curricular activities in PE that can provide a range of different opportunities for children. Some children need to be encouraged to attend. For some the need to get involved in competitive intramural or inter-school activities will enhance and extend their learning. Others may wish to take part in 'club' activities for fun or at more gentle levels of competition. Some will want to take part in creative activities and ones that help develop their fitness and well-being. Schools might consider how it is best to provide opportunities for as many children as possible that will promote higher activity levels, develop their skilfulness and enable them to be challenged. Schools need to recognise the effect that engagement in activity out of lessons has on children's skilfulness, confidence, self-esteem and feelings of competence.

Schools should encourage children to attend clubs in the community to enhance their experiences. Schools need to develop good links with local providers and local authority sport development officers. If schools are promoting links with specific providers and groups, they must ensure that the provision is safe and the quality of provision good. Enormous benefits can be derived from good communication and links.

Play and break times can provide exceptional opportunities for children to practise and extend their skills. As much as 25 per cent of a child's time is spent in the playground during the years at primary school. Where the playground is set up so that purposeful activities that help children's learning are organised, not only the skill level of many children, but also their behaviour is improved. In schools that have adopted policies of this type, a range of resources and ideas are set out from which children can choose. Midday supervisors, teachers, assistant teachers and older children are given the roles of organising and overseeing the activities, and children have the opportunity for focused practice and play. Activities need not be limited to practical or physical skill development. There can also be creative and imaginative play, reading, sand play and so on.

Opportunities to watch, see and closely observe the performance of others can give children a good idea of what they can aspire to. This is most helpful when there are opportunities to talk about what they see and have been involved in.

Practical task

Learning objective: to appreciate that the PE-related learning that goes on in the unstructured context of playtimes is crucial in informing provision.

Log the range of activities that children participate in during one lunchtime period by categorising them under appropriate headings (for example, physical, passive, other). What does this tell you about children's physical abilities, particularly the age group differences?

How can we improve standards in our teaching of PE?

To summarise, and to further assist practitioners in rationalising for themselves the role of the subject, as well as its importance, the question 'What would the school curriculum look like without physical education?' could be posed. Clearly the 'education of the whole child' is not possible without the physical side being addressed and, with that minimal response, what opens up is the debate about purpose, possible content, approach, evaluation of the experience and so forth. Potential and practising teachers need to construct a personal philosophy for the teaching of the subject and be fully aware of the need to revisit and update this as their experience accrues over time and as changes ensue in the education field.

PE is above all an *active* subject, where children can visibly *show immediately* their grasp of a skill or movement without having (necessarily) to wait for feedback. This is why teachers can display their own interest in the subject's contribution to the learning process, by valuing its uniqueness and promoting not just learning for its own sake, but also the extrinsic enjoyment, fun, and reward the subject brings to its participants – for children and teachers alike. By this is meant that *all participants* can benefit from the experiences and opportunities that the subject offers.

PE in the primary school needs to serve a variety of different purposes. Foremost amongst these should be the importance of teaching children about the needs of regular and healthy exercise, the understanding required to identify how important our body is to an active lifestyle, and a respect for the fact that with regular exposure to a breadth and variety of activities, children become increasingly skilled, competent and confident in what their bodies can do. Along the way they should also derive fun and enjoyment through active participation that is physically orientated, contributes to levels of personal fitness, has social dimensions, and is by and large appealing to the majority of children.

In order to teach PE effectively teachers ultimately need to be aware of the key role the subject plays in the all-round development of children during the primary phase of learning. Additionally practitioners in the field require a knowledge base about the subject in order to develop their own confidence in teaching the subject effectively and meet these needs. This process takes time, and can be nurtured through an appreciation of the subject's worth and its natural appeal to children. If there is also enthusiasm, interest and vitality when confronted with the demands of teaching the subject, then it is highly likely that there will be benefits for all engaged in this particular teaching and learning context.

Teaching physical education in the primary school :

a summary of key points

Teachers of primary PE need to:

▬ *examine the nature and purpose of the subject and its place in the education of children in the primary age phase;*

▬ *develop a broad base of knowledge and skills from which they can classify movement in ways relevant to the NC Programmes of Study for Early Years (Foundation) and Key Stages 1 and 2;*

▬ *identify and be able to apply the basic principles underlying the teaching of PE National Curriculum in the primary school with particular reference to dance, games and gymnastic activities, and also for swimming, athletics, and outdoor and adventurous activities as they apply across the age phase.*

To support, help and nurture this, teachers need to:

▬ *engage in an honest and analytical assessment of what they currently know and understand and can do in PE;*

▬ *continue to build upon their personal profile of professional development through in-service training;*

▬ *share ideas and pool knowledge with fellow teachers and professionals;*

▬ *work to ensure that the work undertaken by their children is progressively more challenging and demanding – this is best achieved by regular assessment of children's planning, performance and evaluation skills;*

▬ *ensure that the children have an adequate range of (and opportunity to use) suitable (and appropriate for the activity) materials, equipment and resources when participating in PE activities;*

▬ *consistently push children's learning beyond basic understanding and competence;*

▬ *provide the balance of educational experience within the subject of PE itself and the curriculum generally – recognising in doing so that the subject, beyond its immediate focus on developing locomotor, stability and manipulative competence, also contributes markedly to problem-solving, and related analytic, language and numeracy skills.*

Resources

Core equipment for delivering PE activities

Games – throwing and catching/sending and receiving equipment

Beanbags
Table tennis balls
Shuttlecocks
Sponge balls – assorted shapes, sizes,
  textures, bounce potential
Cricket balls – lightweight, indoor,
  pudding, composition, leather
Sequence/utility balls with symbols,
  numbers, letter markings
Basketballs – micro and mini
Netballs – size 3 and 4
Plastic balls – size 2, 3 and 4
Foam javelins, shot and discus

Balloons
Quoits
Airflow balls
Rubber balls
Rounders balls – plastic, leather
Stoolballs
Softballs
Footballs – size 3 and 4
Rugby balls – size 3 and 4
Tennis balls – low bounce and regular
Hockey balls – indoor and outdoor
Pucks – plastic

Games – striking and fielding equipment

Padder bats – wooden and plastic,
  different shapes, long and short
  handled
Badminton rackets
Shinty sticks
Hockey sticks – range of sizes
Softball bats

Cricket bats – junior sizes
Tennis rackets – short tennis style,
  plastic
Rounders bats
Unihoc sticks
Stoolball bats

Games – miscellaneous

Badminton nets
Marker cones and discs
Wire skittles
Rounders posts
Wooden/plastic canes – for jumping and
  basic hurdling practice
Team braid – primary colours
Kwik Cricket set
Short tennis set
Mini athletics set
Skipping ropes – various lengths
Ball pump(s) and adaptors
Stopwatches
Jumping stands, weighted rope, flexi-bar,
  round section cross bar
Mini basketball posts and nets –
  adjustable heights
Clipboards

Utility stands and posts
Wooden skittles – small and large
Cricket stumps – individual and spring-set
Stoolball posts
Hoops – wooden and plastic, different
  sizes
Team bibs – primary colours
Batinton set
Unihoc set
Marker flags and pegs
Playground chalk
Relay batons
Measuring tapes
Netball posts – adjustable heights
Five-a-side soccer goals
Ribbons
Compasses
Containers – trolley, stands, nets, bags,
  boxes, crates

Gymnastic equipment

Fixed apparatus – window frames, 'cave' type with additional ladders, bars, poles and hoop attachments

Mats – various shapes and sizes, weight and thickness conducive to the age range

Wooden planks – hook attachments at both ends

Nesting tables – ideally five, from 80 cm progressing higher

Wooden stools – various heights

Beat boards – ideally two different types

Set of rope pulleys – also rope ladders, rings

Benches – short and long, plain and padded, with hook attachments, preferably at both ends

Agility table – round or hexagonal, padded top

Bar box – two sections

Section box – three sections

Balance beams – low to floor

Foam equipment – various shapes and sizes

Other everyday PE equipment can also be used for essential basic skills practices, like skipping ropes, jumping canes, skittles, beanbags and cones.

Dance/movement equipment

Access to a good quality sound system (for CD and cassette), appropriate recorded music, and a good range of percussion instruments are all necessary resources to support teaching and learning in this area of the PE curriculum. Poetry and fiction books will lend additional ideas and stimulation to lessons as will visual aids like pictures and posters. Themes and topics central to overall class planning will provide lots of movement ideas too. The use of ribbons and scarves, feathers and balloons – materials and objects that illustrate movement potential – will further support such sessions.

Further reading

Bailey, R. and Macfadyen, T. (2000) *Teaching Physical Education 5-11*. London: Continuum. Provides a good general backcloth to the challenge of teaching PE in the age phase.

Chedzoy, S. (1996) *Physical Education for Teachers and Coordinators at Key Stages 1 and 2*. London: David Fulton. A sound handbook type of book with the emphasis on ensuring that provision is in line with statutory requirements, and guidance on assisting teachers and coordinators in teaching, planning and assessing the subject.

Coates, B. (2000) *Improving Performance in Physical Education KS1 Scheme of Work*. (Coates). Up-to-date guidance and detailed planning formats for delivering the PE curriculum at Key Stage 1.

Coates, B. (2000) *Improving Performance in Physical Education KS2 Scheme of Work*. (Coates). As above, but for Key Stage 2.

Davies, A. and Sabin, V. (1995) *Body Work; Primary Children, Dance and Gymnastics*. Cheltenham: Stanley Thornes. Excellent teaching guidance, clearly linking learning across dance and gymnastics.

DfEE (1999) *Physical Education in the National Curriculum*. London: DFEE and QCA.

DfES (2000) *Curriculum Guidance for the Foundation Stage*. London: DFES and QCA.

Gallahue, D.L. and Ozmun, J. (1998) *Understanding Motor Development – Infants, Children, Adolescents, Adults*. Dubuque, Iowa: McGraw-Hill. Theoretical book promoting a developmental approach to teaching and learning in PE.

Hooper, B., Grey, J. and Maude, T. (2000) *Teaching Physical Education in the Primary School*. London: Routledge. An up-to-date, easy to read resource covering all aspects of teaching PE in the age phase.

Manners, H.K. and Carroll, M.E. (1995) *A Framework for Physical Education in the Early Years*. London: Falmer Press. Addressing PE from an Early Years perspective. Activities and approach advocated here are very child-centred and strong on emphasising the building-blocks strategy for learning.

PEAUK, BAALPE, NDTA (1995) *Teaching Physical Education, Key Stages 1 and 2*. PEAUK, BAALPE, NDTA.

QCA (2000) *Schemes of Work for Physical Education*. London: QCA.

SCAA (1997) *Expectations in Physical Education at Key Stages 1 and 2*. London: SCAA.

Severs, J. (1991) *Activities For PE Using Small Apparatus*. Oxford: Blackwell. Practical guidance on using traditional and commonplace equipment to promote learning in PE.

Sleap, M. (1981) *Mini-Sport*. London: Heinemann. A definitive text showing how to adapt adult games for children.

Useful websites

British Association of Advisers and Lecturers of Physical Education at www.baalpe.org BAALPE aims to promote and maintain high standards and safe practice in physical education in schools, further education establishments and higher education institutions.

Game Central Station at www.gamecentralstation.com Aimed specifically at teachers and parents, contains over 350 searchable games for all ages, many appropriate for PE lesson content.

Physical Education Association of the United Kingdom at www.pea.co.uk The PE Professional Association and publisher of the *British Journal of Teaching Physical Education*. Provides contemporary news and articles as well as useful resources updates.

PE Central at www.pe.central.vt.edu A US site with an excellent quantity and quality of information available. PE teachers send in tips and ideas and the range of lesson ideas is vast.

PE Links at www.pelinks4u.org As above, another US site, with up-to-date news of the PE world. Teachers regularly contribute ideas for day-to-day teaching. Additionally, the site often features various creative initiatives to bolster participation in PE activities and recreation generally.

PE Primary at www.peprimary.co.uk Excellent site for resources to support PE teaching.

Sport England at www.sportengland.org A well organised site where you can download various policy documents and a publications list, along with details of the Sportsmark awards for successful PE teaching.

The importance of music

(adapted from QCA rationale for inclusion in the National Curriculum, 1999)

Music is a powerful, unique form of communication that can change the way pupils feel, think and act.

- *It brings together intellect and feeling and enables personal expression, reflection and emotional development.*
- *As an integral part of culture, past and present, it helps pupils understand themselves and relate to others, forging important links between the home, school and the wider world.*
- *It increases self-discipline and creativity, aesthetic sensitivity and fulfilment.*

Pupils:

- *develop ability to listen and appreciate a wide variety of music and to make judgements about musical quality;*
- *are actively involved in different forms of amateur music making, both individual and communal, developing a sense of group identity and togetherness.*

The purpose of this chapter is not to re-run information that is well presented in the National Curriculum documents, the QCA schemes of work or other curriculum resources designed to provide lesson activities and units of work. Instead, its purpose is to take the starting points that every trainee teacher brings to music teaching and to provide accessible first steps into teaching music backed up by information, suggestions and advice.

Professional values

How would you describe yourself musically? Your own sense of musical identity will have been built up from many experiences of music, in the family, with friends, at school and beyond in the community. There is a commonly held idea that 'being musical' is defined by a set of formal musical skills – being able to 'sing in tune', being able to play an instrument and read music. And there is a strong belief that being able to learn these formal skills is dependent on genetic inheritance, on being born 'musical'. Plenty of research shows that everyone is musically competent and that everyday experience of music is more important in determining whether children become musically confident and competent or not (see, for example, Special Issue of the *Psychologist*, 1994, Is Everyone Musical?). In other cultures, the belief is equally strong that *everyone* is musical; in musical cultures from regions of the African continent for example.

But everyday ideas about musicality being a gift which only a few possess hold firm, even in the face of convincing evidence and ideas from other cultures which contradict or challenge these ideas. Many will adamantly declare that they are 'completely unmusical' or even 'tone deaf'. Often these are firmly held convictions because they have been associated with feelings of failure and humiliation, unfortunately experienced most frequently in school music situations. You may recognise experiences from your own background which were formative in shaping your musical identity.

Trainee teachers I have worked with bring a wealth and diversity of formal and informal musical experiences and expertise. Rarely, however, do they value the whole range of their skills and knowledge because many lie outside the narrow band of skills normally associated with 'being musical'. Consider some typical music experiences and the skills and knowledge they represent.

- Cara taught herself to play guitar and belonged to a band at school. They used to practise in her friend's bedroom and made up their own songs.
- Omma watches a lot of Asian films and is very knowledgeable about songs from the films and the singers.
- Aisha's family were regular attenders at her local church and she sung in the gospel choir from a young age.
- Emma has a keyboard linked to computer software at home and in her spare time she likes to improvise and make up pieces in New Age style.
- Jan's family came from Croatia and he is very interested in the folk music of his country of origin and has an extensive collection of CDs.

So, reconsider your own experiences, interests and enthusiasms for music and see these as the starting point in developing your music teaching.

'Trainees should improve their own teaching, by evaluating it ... they should be motivated and able to take increasing responsibility for their own professional development'

Practical task

Learning objective: to reflect on how music features in your everyday life.
- *Do you have a collection of music to listen to?*
- *What music do you choose to listen to and for what purposes?*
- *What styles of music do you choose and how knowledgeable are you about these?*
- *What different kinds of musical activities do you take part in – as part of home life, social occasions, religious occasions, other festivities?*
- *What role do you take in the musical activities – listener, dancer, music technician, player, singer?*
- *What skills do you have as a listener, dancer, technician, player, singer?*
- *How could some of your own expertise, skills and knowledge for music form starting points for working with children in music?*
- *What would you identify as areas to develop in order to teach music effectively?*

The following example of classroom practice shows how a trainee teacher used her own musical interests as a starting point for an activity about different styles of music and personal music collections.

Classroom story

A trainee teacher brought her own music collection of Irish folk music and played samples of her music to the children. She talked about the different performers and the different styles in her collection and gave the children some general information about Irish folk music. She invited two other adults in the school, an administrator and another teacher, to also bring, play and talk about their music collections to the children. One collection was of Romantic opera and the other a collection of Cliff Richard songs going right back to some early records. For homework the children were asked to interview two adults, family or friends, about their own music – music collections they have or music they know and remember from their past.

The following week the trainee teacher organised a circle time listening and discussion session when the children talked about what they had found out from their interviews and some different pieces of music loaned by family members were listened to. She encouraged discussion about the music itself, about its time and its place and about its significance to the person to whom the music belonged.

'Trainees should have high expectations of all pupils, respect their social, cultural, linguistic, religious and ethnic backgrounds and be committed to raising their educational achievement'

Music is closely associated with who we are and our place in the world. Music carries strong messages of identity, particularly social, cultural and ethnic. Think of the music, movement and costumes at the Notting Hill Carnival, at a folk festival in Cornwall or at a state ceremonial occasion. Music plays important and different roles in religion; for some devout Muslims, for example, there are restrictions on the listening and playing of music, in other religions there are special types of music which carry important spiritual meanings. I once received a request from the parent of a Palestinian boy not to repeat an Israeli song we had sung. Music is loaded with meanings of which we all need to be aware.

'Trainees should contribute to, and share responsibly in, the corporate life of the school'

Music plays an important part in collective occasions in primary schools. Song-singing in particular is a communal activity which brings everyone together. Taking part in assembly and joining in the singing give important messages about your commitment to the corporate life of the school.

'Trainees should understand the contribution that support staff and other professionals make to teaching and learning'

Many schools employ visiting teachers for music, usually to teach instrumental lessons to individuals or groups of children and sometimes to take curriculum music. These teachers are often peripatetic teachers who will be less familiar with the school routines, will know the children less well and so on. Liaising with and supporting these staff will help to ensure that their teaching goes smoothly. There may be ways that you can integrate the work of instrumental teachers and the children who receive lessons in the work of the whole class; they are often happy to lead short demonstration and performance sessions with their instruments. With curriculum music, trainee teachers should attend and participate in the lessons on at least some occasions in order to develop their own music teaching and to support the visiting teachers. It is often a valuable opportunity to observe the children in your class working with another teacher.

'Trainees should have high expectations for all pupils and be committed to raising their educational achievement'

When the National Curriculum was first introduced it carried the expectation that all primary schools would teach music to all children. At the same time it became the responsibility of class teachers to ensure that a broad and balanced music curriculum was being provided for all the children in their class. This inclusiveness – both for children and for teachers – may seem obvious, but until that time music teaching in primary schools had been patchy, with some schools providing active and lively music teaching and some none at all. The National Curriculum requirements also spelt out the kinds of activities in which children should now be involved. It was organised around the three core activities of 'composing, performing and listening'. Whereas primary school music had been dominated by singing, particularly communal singing (and still is to a large extent), all children were expected to have opportunities to compose their own music, to listen to a wide range of music and to gain musical knowledge and skills.

Although the ideal of music taught by all teachers to all children is embodied in the National Curriculum, in practice this is much more difficult to achieve. Of all the arts subjects in the primary school, because of the belief that to teach music you must have specialist skills, music has tended to be either neglected or allocated to a specialist teacher, particularly at Key Stage 2.

Practical task

Learning objective: to consider your observations of music teaching in the classroom.

In your school experience so far, what curriculum music teaching have you observed? Who taught the music – a specialist teacher or the class teacher? What kind of activities did you observe?

Consider carefully what you have observed of music teaching so far. Has it covered the full range of activities – performing, composing, listening to music and investigating music – as set out in the National Curriculum? What messages do the children receive if the class teacher teaches music – in comparison with a specialist teacher? What might be the advantages or disadvantages of generalist or specialist teaching?

You may know schools where there is a lot of musical activity, there are choirs and recorder groups and there are musical concerts and shows at the end of term for parents. It is important that these performance activities which can be the show-case for a school's music are not selective and that all children have equal opportunity to take part. When some children receive extra musical tuition in the form of instrumental lessons, choirs and music groups beyond the school curriculum then by the end of Key Stage 2 there may be considerable variety in the abilities of all the children. While valuing variety and allowing for a wide range of musical pathways, it is important to ensure that all children have the chance to develop their potential.

Knowledge and understanding

In the first section I attempted to show how trainee teachers usually measure up how competent they feel in music against a set of formal musical skills and to downgrade what they have gained both from in-school and out-of-school musical experiences. Consequently, many trainee teachers underestimate how much knowledge and understanding they bring to music teaching. The first practical task asked you to consider your musical identity and background. Now it is valuable to carry out a more specific audit of your musical knowledge and understanding.

Practical task

Learning objective: to assess your own musical knowledge and understanding.

Look at the music audit in Chapter 6 and read through the first section: Knowledge and Understanding. In the sections 'Evidence', describe your prior achievements and then set out what you might work on and how. It could be that you will dust off your clarinet from the attic, take a sudden interest in your partner's collection of medieval music or practise singing along to children's song tapes in the car.

In the sections that follow, various areas of skill and knowledge for music are considered.

Core skills

LISTENING

Working in music with children is, fundamentally, about teaching them to listen sensitively, perceptively and knowledgeably. This is the core skill that underpins all musical activity in listening to music, performing and composing. Listening is also a transferable skill which assists learning across the whole curriculum. In primary schools, particularly with the youngest ages, a very high proportion of learning is achieved aurally by children listening to and understanding what is said. Some children who find it difficult to settle and to listen with concentration can be helped in a general way with all their learning if they are taught to be good listeners. An activity that aims to focus and develop children's ability to listen with concentration and perception might precede learning activities in other curriculum areas.

Teachers need to be good listeners, too. For the teaching of music it is essential to be able to listen, remember and quickly evaluate children's work in sound as it is produced. Listening to children well is also a key skill of teaching – the kind of listening that not only picks up what children say with accuracy but also conveys to them that you value their contributions. This helps the making of good relationships with children.

Practical task

Learning objective: to pilot a listening activity in the classroom.

The following classroom activity is intended for children and can be adapted for almost any age. Try it out with instruments, or found sound-makers, before you work with children.

Listening game

Learning objectives:

- *to listen with concentration;*
- *to control the sound-makers to produce just one sound;*
- *to be able to reproduce sounds aurally;*
- *to describe sounds using their own words.*

Step 1
The children sit in a circle. Set out in the centre of the circle is a collection of six or seven untuned percussion instruments. Begin by listening – just listen – what sounds do you hear around you now? Wait for quiet.

Step 2
One child moves into the centre of the circle, chooses one instrument, makes one tiny sound with it and replaces it. She chooses a second child who must imitate her first sound as exactly as possible and then make a second tiny sound with another instrument. The game continues – a third child must replicate the first two sounds as closely as possible and add a third – and so on.

This game encourages the children to listen with concentration and to focus their listening on single sounds. When a next child attempts to reproduce a sound, it is automatic to make a comparison with an aural memory of the original sound – was it a little louder, quieter, longer?

Step 3
Ask the children to explain the slight differences they hear between different versions of the sounds. They will hear these very accurately but their ability to describe this in words will depend on how experienced they are at using musical vocabulary. Their ability to use musical terms will depend on their prior learning.

Extension

You might take this opportunity to talk about some specific aspects of the sounds made from the instruments such as:

- *ways of playing each instrument (struck, shaken, plucked);*
- *how the sound can be varied on each instrument – made louder, softer, longer, shorter;*
- *those instruments which have more resonance where the sound lasts, and those instruments which are non-resonant when the sound is dry and short;*
- *a comparison of the pitch of different instruments – higher or lower than;*
- *the timbre of the instruments using descriptive vocabulary such as jingly, ringing, sharp, hollow.*

Introduce a discussion about the instruments themselves, touching on:

- *what they are called;*
- *the materials they are made of;*
- *how they are constructed;*
- *where they come from.*

UNDERSTANDING MUSICAL TERMS

Although it is useful in the course of this section on knowledge and understanding to look at some key musical terms, the National Curriculum document stresses that the raw materials of music, the elements, processes and skills, cannot be separated out from their use in musical contexts. That is, the terms only make sense when applied and used in musical situations. So, for example, if we consider the term 'pulse' – the steady beat which underpins most music – the pulse of a military march has quite a different feel to it than the pulse of a salsa dance. The feel of the pulse is integrated with all the other features of the music – the tone of the instruments, the way the melody moves, the texture of the music and how loud the music is.

So while there are some common features about the basic elements of music as they occur in different kinds of music, be wary of teaching musical terms such as 'pulse' as if they were something which can be isolated from musical experiences. Many schemes of work over the last few years have tended to adopt a separated-out approach. Looking through them you will find individual units which cover the single elements such as 'pitch', 'rhythm pattern', 'dynamics' and so on. The Schemes of Work published by the QCA encourage a more integrated approach. As a general strategy, aim to introduce the basic materials of music by drawing them out of real musical examples - recorded music, songs, the children's compositions – encountering them again and again in different musical situations.

In my experience, trainee teachers have no difficulty with understanding and working with the basic musical materials such as dynamics (loud and soft), tempo (fast and slow), duration (long sounds, short sounds) and so on. Timbre, the actual sound, the tone quality of the instrument is a more unusual term. And texture is a term commonly used to describe the density of the music, whether there is just one instrument playing or a whole band. The distinction between pulse (or steady beat) and the rhythmic patterning of a piece of music can be confusing. The pulse provides the regularly timed underpinning around which the rhythm patterns are organised. Find the pulse by tapping along to the music. The rhythm will be framed by the beat but is made up of patternings of subdivisions of the beats and longer durations of more than one beat length. Usually the rhythm is found by tapping out the main melody. To complicate matters, there may be more complex rhythmic patterning inside the texture of the music.

Using the voice

Although obvious, it is a little emphasised fact that all teachers are professional voice users. All day they communicate vocally. How you use your voice can convey not only the information the children need, but also how you feel towards them and about teaching them. We all know from our own experiences of being taught how lessons from one teacher could be dull and monotonous and from another teacher full of life and interest, making you want to listen and participate. The emotional tenor of the class, whether the children feel positive about themselves and in turn about working with you, is conveyed in the way you use your voice. The management of behaviour is also largely dependent on effective communication through voice and body language. So what does this have to do with music? Using your voice expressively, with good timing and intonation (the way the pitch of the voice rises and falls) is, in essence, musical. Knowing how to use your voice with a good technique, so that you don't tire or even damage your voice – both common complaints in the early days of teaching – links voice use as a performance skill for music and drama with voice use for teaching in general.

Experienced teachers have a repertoire of vocal styles that they use for different kinds of communication with children. Many of these voice styles are only used in teaching and need to be consciously learned by trainee teachers. In your first school experience you may find these communication styles unfamiliar and consciously have to practise your 'teaching voices', but they soon become second nature.

Practical task

Learning objective: to experiment with using your voice in a range of tones and inflections to express different emotions.

Can you sound surprised, assertive, excited, disappointed? When in school, listen carefully to the way teachers use their voice when giving instructions, when checking children's behaviour, when addressing the whole class in quite a large room or just talking to individuals, and so on. Experiment with and practise these different voice styles.

Projecting the voice to fill the space of a classroom requires a certain technique and can be tiring on the voice at first. Some simple tips are to avoid dehydration, which will affect the vocal folds (not too much coffee at breaktime), remember to stand well, to breathe well and to feel relaxed, particularly in the throat, upper chest and shoulders.

Some activities in music, drama and language work will require specific vocal techniques. Obviously singing is one and we will come to this. Perhaps less obvious are the rhythmical and melodic way the voice might be used in storytelling, rhyming and rapping. Changing the tone and timbre of the voice will add to the effect. As with anything in teaching, particularly the performance arts, you will set a model for the children. They should be encouraged to use their voices well - whatever the context and the activity, clear pronunciation, good diction, expressive and rhythmic delivery will be important.

Singing

You are probably someone who enjoys singing and sings with confidence. On the other hand you may be one of the unfortunately many people for whom the thought of singing to a class of children is not a happy prospect.

Firstly it is important to recognise that singing is an ability which is learned. There is no evidence of the ability to sing being 'in the genes' – however strongly you may have been led to believe that, it is just not the case. What is certain is that ours is not a culture which encourages everyday singing. Indeed, singing is often the butt of jokes and people tend to mock their own voices. This is in striking contrast to the importance of singing in popular music.

Whatever your level of confidence as a singer, there are some straightforward ways in which you can get started and improve your singing voice. These ways are useful to hand on to the children you teach and they will provide a good repertoire of warm-up activities to precede singing activities in your teaching. They are also a very useful strategy for calming and focusing a class.

POSTURE
Good posture will ensure good breathing. Standing, as opposed to sitting, will improve the posture for singing. It can make a surprising difference to the singing sound just to ask everyone to stand. The tradition of sitting children cross-legged on the floor for assembly encourages a rounded-back posture which is not conducive to good singing.

- **Stand upright, not stiffly, head held up.**
- **Stand with the feet spaced slightly apart, hands loosely by the side or clasped in front.**
- **Rotate the shoulders, bring them up to the ears and drop them again, tip the head gently from side to side. Repeat each of these exercises a few times in a slow and relaxed way.**
- **Gently push the shoulders back so that the rib cage is opened out.**

BREATHING
A generous flow of air through the vocal folds will develop a full singing tone and automatically improve the quality of the sound. Asking children to simply 'sing up' can be counter-productive resulting in a hoarse, strained, out-of-tune sound.

- **Breathe deeply using the whole lung capacity.**
- **Encourage controlled breathing and awareness of the diaphragm.**

- **Place both hands on each side of the lower rib cage to feel the expansion and contraction of the rib cage in breathing. Then pant quickly, laugh or pretend to cough to feel the diaphragm in action.**

Various exercises can develop breath control.

- **Hold a finger about 10 to 20 centimetres from the mouth, purse the lips and blow very gently onto the finger.**
- **Breathe in deeply and blow out with one strong puff. Children can pretend to 'blow out the candles on a birthday cake'.**

VOWEL SOUNDS

Using the mouth energetically, enunciating the words clearly with good diction will ensure that the words of songs are communicated. Open vowel sounds carry the singing tone.

- **Loosen up the mouth parts by rubbing the cheeks and exercising the jaw. Children can pretend to 'chew a toffee'. They enjoy pulling and pushing their mouths to sing with 'funny voices' and 'squashy voices'.**
- **On one single pitch, ask the children to sing through the vowel sounds – aah, ay, i, oh, ooo. Be conscious of lip shapes and the back of the throat relaxing into each vowel sound.**
- **Sing syllable sounds repeatedly – ma, ma, ma, ma, moo, moo – and so on, to improve diction. See how fast they can be articulated.**

There are obvious links between these activities and other aspects of musical learning, with pitch, with volume, with rhythm.

Consciously vary the pitch of your singing voice. Can you sing the vowel sounds with the upper register of your voice and then with the lower register? Feel the difference. Explore your voice; slide up and down in pitch. Now experiment with volume. To sing very quietly requires good breath control. Now attempt to vary the dynamics. The syllable sounds can be practised to rhythm patterns, the sort of jazzy 'doobie, doo' sounds are a good start.

With children there are not only extensions from voice techniques into learning about the musical elements, there are also close links with phonic work in literacy. Practising clear diction of phonic sounds will help children to hear and distinguish them clearly. Chanting and singing them will help to reinforce their learning.

Song repertoire

All teachers need to acquire a repertoire of songs that they can use with their classes for specific music learning purposes. Songs and rhymes are also useful for more general purposes in the day-to-day management of a class of children. They can occupy waiting times, they can help to organise the children or to create a sense of community as a class. One reception class teacher must take her children down a long corridor to the hall for assembly. A train song enables them to 'chuff' along to the hall in a line at a brisk pace. Some class teachers have songs to begin or end the day. One trainee teacher from New Zealand ended every day with a Maori song from his home. The children sensed that it was special to him and enjoyed the security and ritual of singing it every day at 'home time'.

If you haven't sung for a while, or are unsure of yourself as a singer, the massed singing times in schools, particularly assembly, are a good opportunity to find your singing voice again. A repertoire of songs for singing with children at Foundation and Key Stage I can be quickly learned in most schools by joining in with singing occasions in the nursery or classroom. Almost all publications of songs for primary music now carry a CD which presents a recorded version of the song. These provide a useful resource from which you can learn an appropriate repertoire of songs for use in teaching. Practise any songs you are going to teach the children thoroughly so that you know the melody and all the words very well.

Playing instruments

You may be a competent instrumentalist or you may have never played an instrument in your life. Many trainee teachers are lapsed players of the recorder, the piano or other orchestral instruments that they learned in school. All these experiences give you an insight into the techniques and skills required to perform on instruments. You will know that there are specific ways to hold, to blow, to strike, to scrape or to shake instruments so that they make the sound you want. You will also know that it takes differing degrees of control and physical dexterity with fingers, hands and arms to produce sounds.

In music lessons which are taught as part of the mainstream curriculum – in contrast to instrumental lessons which are usually taught outside the mainstream curriculum – children are given opportunities to play a range of instruments. These are, in most instances, instruments that have come to be traditionally used in education because the technique to play them is relatively simple. You have probably experienced them in your own education – percussion instruments, recorders and more recently keyboards. There are particular types of barred instruments that are widespread in schools. They are tuned - xylophones (with wooden keys), metallophones (with resonant, matt metal keys) and glockenspiels (with metal keys, a bright sound and usually smaller in size). These are known as Orff instruments, named after the composer Carl Orff who in Germany in the 1920s initiated an approach to music education based on the use of these tuned percussion instruments.

Even though the technique to produce sound from percussion instruments might appear relatively simple, there are some principles to follow in playing them well. Whether tapping with a beater or striking with a hand, a crisp movement that bounces off the surface will produce a clear sound. Often children leave the beater or their hand resting on the instrument instead of rebounding. Many wooden instruments will resonate richly if held lightly in just a way that allows the sound to ring. It is also important to have a range of beaters – or mallets as they are termed – made from different materials; rubber, felt, wood, soft fibres, plastic, in different hardnesses and different sizes. Which beater to use is often a matter of experiment, preference and what sounds right for the musical purpose.

Practical task

Learning objective: to become familiar with the range of musical instruments available.

Look through school equipment catalogues at the instruments available or research one of the books which gives information about instruments using the references at the end of this chapter. Take particular note of the names of the instruments. If you have access to a percussion instrument, use this, or find some improvised sound makers.

Explore some techniques for playing your instrument. Listen very alertly to the sound. How can you achieve what you consider to be the best sound? If you have the opportunity to watch live performers playing percussion, take particular note of their playing technique.

Notation

The National Curriculum side-steps the issue of whether children should learn to read and write conventional staff notation – the lines and black dots of music. It refers to 'relevant established and invented notations' at Key Stage 2.

In thinking about notation, it is worth remembering that the majority of music in the world is not written down, but is made, performed and passed on through aural processes. Folk musicians in Ireland gather in pubs and learn melodies by listening and playing along with others – much the same process by which songs are learnt aurally in school. Pop musicians learn much of their early repertoire by listening repeatedly and imitating recordings by artists they like and admire. Again, the emphasis in Western art music has been on musical processes which focus on written versions of the music, but with the broadening of the music curriculum to encompass all kinds of music, notation perhaps becomes less central. There is certainly a feeling among many music educators that an emphasis on reading from the dots can result in children who are less competent at aural processes such as improvisation, learning music by ear and so on. At the same time, contemporary technologies are diminishing the need for notation systems. Music can be made on computers, stored on cassette or other forms of technological memory and performed by the same means. Recent computer programs can convert played music into notation, if required, automatically.

So it is important to consider what the advantages of written notation are. Notation enables performers to reproduce music composed by other people and for the music to be distributed widely. The process of composing using notations probably allows longer, more complex and intricately worked out pieces of music to be composed than would be possible through aural processes alone.

Looking at all sides of the notation issue, there is a mystique that surrounds the ability to read conventional music notation. In the introduction I mentioned those skills which are usually associated with feeling competent musically. Being able to read music is one of them. It may be important to dispel this mystique by giving every child access to conventional notation as one of a range of musical processes that they can use when relevant and appropriate. Currently, the situation exists in many schools whereby some children receive instrumental tuition, but not all. These children learn notation in their instrumental lessons resulting in very differentiated skills for music among children, particularly by the end of Key Stage 2.

Many teacher trainees will have been introduced to staff notation at some stage in their education and just need to refresh their memories. If you have no prior experience, skip on to the section on teaching and work through the classroom activity which is intended as an introduction to staff notation.

Knowledge of recorded music

Think of any one of the major music stores. The rack upon rack of different kinds of music are a reminder of the wealth of music available for listening to now. Children should be introduced to a broad range of music and so it is important that you extend your own knowledge of music. The range will be representative of different times, music from different historical periods – and places, music from different cultures of the world – and music for different purposes, lullabies, hymns, marches, dances and so on. The music stores usefully categorise the racks of CDs according to style of music, country of origin and so on. Browsing is a good way to extend your knowledge of the enormous range of music that we can listen to now.

Practical task

Learning objective: to develop your knowledge of music beyond your own listening repertoire.

*Select some music with which you are less familiar – from a library or from a friend's collection. The **Rough Guides to Music** with their accompanying CDs are a good resource to use for this activity (Broughton et al, 1994). Alternatively the internet provides useful sources of musical information with sound clips of the music itself.*

- *Listen to the music carefully to get to know it.*
- *Try to set aside any personal preferences and listen to the music objectively.*
- *Listen to the music repeatedly. This is important as first impressions can be misleading.*
- *Find out as much about the music as you can from reading or from internet sources.*

MUSIC OF THE PAST

All music has a history, yet conventionally in education *the* history of music has been confined to music composed by male European composers of so-called 'classical' music. The history of music composed by women, non-European ethnic and non-elite social groups has not been preserved, recorded or included in educational curricula. The history of Western European art music is defined by period: Early music, Medieval music, Baroque music (Handel, Bach), Classical (Mozart, Beethoven), Romantic (Tchaikowsky, Rachmaninov), Contemporary.

The term 'classical' music is often used loosely and broadly to describe music which is not pop, but specifically refers to a period of music history between roughly the end of the sixteenth century and the end of the eighteenth century.

WORLD MUSICS

The term 'world music' is criticised as emphasising unhelpful divisions between different styles of music – between the dominant styles of North American and European music and 'other' musics, defined collectively as 'world musics'. To avoid this bias, endeavour to describe music accurately by its specific country, region, people, town of origin.

FOLK AND TRADITIONAL MUSICS

Folk and traditional musics are often collected under world musics. The distinction has arisen in European musics because of the strong tradition of art music that has separated from the traditions of folk music. It is important to recognise that many cultures of music have 'high' and 'low', or folk forms. Folk music is often associated with the ways of life among the rural and working classes.

JAZZ

Jazz is another generic term that covers a very wide range of different styles from traditional to contemporary. Jazz style developed at the end of the nineteenth century in America. Improvisation is a key process in jazz.

POPULAR STYLES

Although Anglo-American popular music styles have dominated, elements of popular style have been incorporated into many culturally diverse musics. The cross-mixing of styles is leading to interesting variety. Commercial processes of production, presentation and promotion are central and defining in popular music.

Ways of listening

There are different ways of listening to music associated with different styles of music. Concert hall listening – that is, to listen in silence and stillness – is appropriate for some styles of music, mostly from the Western European art music tradition. This is the way of listening to music that has been imported into music education and is often called 'music appreciation'. But it is not the way we listen to most music. Jazz, pop, folk music and music from different cultures, all have settings within which they are most likely to be performed and ways of listening which fit with those settings. Many audiences will expect to join in with the performance in some way, to engage with the music by moving, dancing, clapping, singing along or by responding with calls and shouts to the players. In other words, sitting still and in silence is the exception rather than the norm if we consider the full spectrum of music listening styles. For children, particularly younger children, it can be very demanding to sit and listen to music for an extended length of time. That said, we should not underestimate children's ability to listen with rapt attention for long periods of time to music that has held their interest.

Teaching

Planning

The National Curriculum requirements were carefully designed and written to be accessible to all. In addition, a large number of publications to support primary music teaching have been published including a Scheme of Work for Key Stages 1 and 2 by the Qualifications and Curriculum Authority (QCA, 2000). These publications aim to demystify music, to provide practical and easily usable resource materials. You should find and look at some of these resource materials in order to develop your own music teaching. A selection is listed in the resources section of this chapter.

Music is traditionally taught as a whole class lesson very much directed by the teacher. The lesson often takes more the form of a rehearsal session in which new songs are learned, known ones practised a little more and some old favourites revisited. This may be the kind of lesson you are familiar with. In addition there may be listening and talking about some recorded music, and there may be an opportunity for children to create their own music.

In this kind of lesson the teacher has an active, lead role and the children a passive, follower role. Children learn best when they are able to actively engage, to contribute their own ideas and to be fully active in the processes that are central to music. The traditional music lesson centred on singing may not leave much room for children's own ideas and contributions. Compare this model of music teaching with the way that art, for example, is generally taught. Here the teacher expects the children to be very active in creating their own art, in working with materials and exploring the processes.

You may have been fortunate in your own schooling and in your experience of schools up until now to have experienced and observed good models of teaching in which children were all engaged in creative and active music-making. But this is probably the exception rather than the norm. Getting started in teaching music is, then, probably also about trying to imagine how music could be taught differently. Imagining this can be difficult if you have only experienced limited versions of music education in your own school and from what you have observed in your experience of schools so far.

Listening to recorded music

Listening to and investigating recorded music is a key strand of the music curriculum. In general, it is a strand that is not developed by class teachers as much as it might be. This is surprising for, in my view, it is one of the most accessible ways to introduce music teaching and learning into the classroom. For this reason I am looking in some detail at planning based on recorded music.

Playing recorded music in the classroom can integrate well with day-to-day activities. There might be quiet and soothing music playing when children arrive in the morning to help settle them in to school. There might be music to accompany various activities such as changing for games or tidying up. It can also be useful at moments when the children need to calm or relax or as an alternative to storytime. There is some evidence that playing recorded music can be an additional tool in behaviour management.

Some schools have organised a listening repertoire of recorded music to accompany the children's leading in and leading out of the hall for assembly. While this is a good way to increase the amount and variety of music which the children are hearing, their ability to listen to music purposefully also needs to be extended. There are a number of purposes for using recorded music, some of them directly connected with their learning objectives in the music curriculum, some of them broader.

- **To extend children's knowledge of different music of different times, places and styles.**
- **To develop children's perception and understanding of the elements of music and how they work together in music.**
- **As a source of ideas for children's own music-making, for example, as a starting point for composition or to listen for how music is performed.**
- **To connect with their work in other areas of the curriculum, with art, science, history, dance and geography.**
- **To enhance the everyday life of the classroom or whole school, for example, to calm the class or give a sense of formal gathering for assembly.**

DANCE LISTENING

Dance and music share many of the same features. The two activities fit well together, enhancing children's learning in both curriculum areas. The children can learn dance forms that combine with dance music or make up their own dances to music. Here are some suggested activities.

- *Place*. **The children learn traditional dances accompanied by the appropriate music, e.g. from specific geographical regions of the UK.**
- *Time*. **The children listen to dance music from a particular period of history, e.g. a Baroque minuet. They research the dances and either make up their own or learn exact versions.**
- *Style*. **The children study art dance forms from different cultures and look at the connections between the dance and music, e.g. European classical ballet, South Indian karnatic dances.**
- *Purpose*. **The children find out about music and dances for celebrating, e.g. harvest celebrations.**
- *Techniques*. **The children focus on specific techniques, e.g. 'shoe' dancing in an Irish clog-dancing workshop given by a visiting performer and then go on to look at other 'shoe' dancing such as Stomp, tap-dancing, wellie boot dancers from South Africa. The toe-tapping rhythms are worked on in dance and then listened to with focus in the music.**

At some point focus the children's attention on the music alone. This may be in the start-up session, as an interim, or during a plenary session.

PERFORMANCE LISTENING

Joining in with the music by playing or singing with it enables the children to 'get inside' it and helps them to learn how the music works. Children often mime the actions of performers when they listen to music and this activity can be encouraged and extended.

- Play a recorded version of a song the children already know, e.g. a folk song or nursery rhyme. They listen, sing along and then discuss the performer's style of singing in comparison with their own.
- Choose recorded music that has a simple, distinctive feature, e.g. a steady beat or pulse played on a drum. The children pick out the feature and clap or tap along.

GAME LISTENING

Game activities to recorded music help to focus the children's attention on specific aspects of the music and also retain their interest and involvement.

- Choose a piece of music with a recurring feature, e.g. trumpets which play alternating sections. The children must stand up when they hear the trumpets and sit down when they stop playing.
- Choose a piece of music with three or four distinctive sections. The children are grouped and each group acts out their section of the music.

IMAGE LISTENING

Children can be asked to visualise aspects of the music and reproduce them on paper. This kind of activity can focus on specific elements of the music, usually pitch or rhythm. In this way the children must listen very attentively for when something happens musically and the detail of how it happens.

- Choose a piece of music with a very simple melody or rhythmic pattern, e.g. a melody which descended slowly by step every now and then. Whenever the children hear this melody they 'draw it' with blobs for each note on large pieces of scrap paper.

Representational drawing can be more problematic. The visual imagery of the drawing can come to dominate, distracting children's attention from the music and on to the art work. In addition, music tends not to be 'about' visual representation – at least, only a very few pieces of music are intended to invoke, pictorially, specific scenes or events. A piece of music might evoke mood and atmosphere, which then feeds the imagination for art work.

Classroom story

A class of Year 4 children were following a theme of fairy-tale characters in literature, art and music. The trainee teacher played the music of 'Gnomus', meaning gnome, from the collection of pieces Pictures at an Exhibition by Mussorgsky, a Russian composer living at the end of the nineteenth century. There are two versions of this music, one for piano and one which was later orchestrated by Ravel, a French composer. The children were invited to improvise dance to the orchestral version. It has rapid movement followed by sudden pauses, then loud heavy chords. These musical features were discussed and represented in movement.

In another session the children listened to the piano version and discussed how it compared with the orchestral version. Although not a pianist herself, the trainee teacher took the children to the piano in the hall and explored with them the very high and low sounds of the piano. She mimicked playing the piano when the music played again – and the children also played 'air piano'.

Next the children researched gnomes and other mythical creatures in fairy-tales, films and other children's stories. They looked at art by Rackman before producing their own art work versions of Gnomus. As part of the process of preparing the art work, they returned to their dance versions of the music. Their paintings were photographed digitally, printed out from the computer, photocopied onto overhead transparencies and projected onto the hall wall to accompany the music and their dancing.

LISTENING AND WRITING

Activities that link listening and writing about the music will develop different aspects of the children's knowledge. They might write as they listen repeatedly or they might listen and then research. Children can look at examples of writing about music in programme notes, in magazines or on CD covers. They could be asked to write:

- **personal impressions of the music;**
- **information gathered from reference sources about the music itself or about the performers;**
- **descriptions of the music using musical terms.**

Planning for singing

Both for Key Stage 1 and Key Stage 2 there is one unit of work in the Scheme of Work (QCA, 2000) described as 'ongoing skills'. This unit of work focuses on singing and the expectation is that this will be a part of the music curriculum that is given continuous attention and practice. The children you teach may be singing almost daily in assembly and have a weekly hymn practice. But this usually happens as a large group activity. Quality teaching of singing is best achieved with class groups and smaller group work.

Earlier in this chapter I stressed that singing is an ability which is learned. Pre-school experiences of being sung to at home and of having their first efforts at singing encouraged and praised will mean that some children have a better start for singing when they arrive in school than others. The low level of awareness among teachers that singing is a skill which needs appropriate support, practice and development means that children may be missing out on the kind of education in singing which they most need. Short, frequent opportunities to practise are ideal. The songs themselves should be well matched to children's current levels of ability as singers.

Classroom story

About two or three times a week a final year BA/QTS trainee teacher on placement in a reception class calls a 'singing register'. She sings the children's names and then asks 'are you here?' on a simple two-note chant that she makes up on the spur of the moment. The children sing back to her on a similar chant, 'Yes, Miss McDonald'. She invites the children to make up their own singing tune in reply. After each child has sung she gives a feedback comment telling them whether they have used their singing voice and whether they made up an interesting melody. For those who are not yet using their singing voice, but half-singing on just a single pitch or even just speaking the words, she asks them to try again.

She ticks their names on the official register but also has a tick list of all their names on which she is recording their progress as singers over the term.

This activity is easily accommodated in the everyday routines of the classroom. It provides regular practice at singing. There are some children in her class who are not clear on the distinction between speaking voice and singing voice. Sarah McDonald gives the children specific feedback on how they are singing. There are some teachers who are nervous of giving children feedback about their singing and singling them out for help because they are concerned it will damage the children's confidence as singers. However, not to provide the children with an opportunity and a rigorous means of learning how to improve their singing will have more long-term detrimental effects, perhaps even denting their confidence permanently. This is, after all, only the basis of good practice in all other curriculum areas. It is the dominant belief that singing is an innate ability that has prevented the development of effective interventions aimed at teaching children to learn to sing.

The repertoire for singing at Key Stage 2 needs to reflect children's increasing interest in a wide range of musical styles, including popular styles. Boys in particular can lose interest in singing at this age. It is important, therefore, that male members of staff, workshops from visiting musicians, video viewings of singers and recordings provide models of men singing. Technology incorporated with singing activities can be a bonus. Amplification equipment, recording and karaoke equipment can all enhance vocal activities and give singing a contemporary edge.

Teaching
Composing

There is a strong recognition in many areas of the curriculum that children need to be engaged in making their own work; in writing poems and stories, in choreographing dances, in drawing, painting, sculpting and model-making. In music, no less, children need to have opportunities to create their own music. They find composition fascinating and absorbing. It gives children a vital opportunity to work with the materials of music and for discovering how music is constructed.

Today we had a group of 4 and 1 of us stared and then the thres second and when the third came in the first stopped and when the last came in the second stopped.
Next I would like to do a xyopore tune with two other people.

The trainee teacher can provide for compositional activity in many ways. One of the most straightforward ways is to provide children with access to the materials of composition – that is, freedom to use their voices, instruments, various technologies for composing and recording – and the time, space and encouragement to make their own music. Young children often need time to make music on their own terms first and would find it difficult to conform to specific compositional starting points. Older children need a balance of prescribed starting points and opportunities to decide their own compositional tasks. They often have definite ideas of the kind of music they would be interested in making and some of the best results arise when they have a fairly free hand.

Starting points which take an imaginative stimulus, a mood or story as ideas to be interpreted in music can seem like the most accessible way in which to approach composition. But in reality, making music in this way can be difficult. Materials, structural ideas and musical processes give children something more concrete to work with. As a result, they find these approaches easier and the outcomes are usually more satisfactory. Some examples might be:

- **make music with a partner, taking turns or synchronising;**
- **make music using a simple set of pitches fixed in advance;**
- **find some rhythm patterns and string them together in sequences;**
- **explore three-note chords and sing a melody over a group of chords.**

A CLASSROOM ACTIVITY
Learning objectives:

- **to improvise rhythm patterns;**
- **to extend the children's techniques for playing untuned percussion instruments;**
- **to perform a simple paired improvisation with a partner.**

Step 1. The children are sitting in a circle and chant the following rhyme, or better still something similar that you or the children make up on the spur of the moment.

'Here I <u>come</u>, here I <u>come</u>, with a <u>rhy</u>thm on my <u>drum</u>'

The stresses fall on the words that are underlined.

Then follow the chant with four claps that keep exactly to the beat at the same tempo.

Step 2. The children chant the rhyme and leave out the following four claps, but leave a silence equivalent to the four beats. They must feel the four beats internally.

Step 3. Hand out one untuned instrument. Something which has two pitches, such as a pair of double-headed bongo drums or a two-tone woodblock, would work well. Two instruments could be handed out, one each at opposite points in the circle.

The class chants the rhyme all together and the child or children with the instruments improvise an interesting rhythm to fill the four-beat gap. Once finished, they immediately pass on the instrument to the next child. With some younger children it may be helpful to first tap out the four beats of the 'gap' on their instrument before going on to make up their own rhythms.

Extension 1. Focus on some of the improvised rhythms by asking individual children to play their pattern for the rest of the class to echo clap. Draw attention to musical features of the rhythms – you played lots of very fast, very quick taps – or that felt very jazzy, very jerky on the bongos. And comment on how easy they were to imitate or whether they required careful listening and were difficult to remember.

These are the key learning points in the lesson where the children are asked to focus, to listen to precise detail of rhythms. Putting into words develops the children's understanding of what they are hearing and doing.

Extension 2. Ask two children to make a conversation of improvised rhythms taking the simple structure – 'your turn, my turn, your turn, my turn'. Giving this four-turn structure prevents the children from 'conversing' endlessly.

Organise the whole class into pairs to make improvised conversations. If instruments are in short supply, the children can work on patterns using body percussion sounds (clapping, tapping knees, clicking etc) and then play what they have made on instruments later.

Bring the class back together for a plenary session. Listen to some conversations performed by pairs of children. This gives children an opportunity to perform to the rest of the class and for children to listen carefully to others playing. Recording the performances introduces a small element of ICT and enables play-back and further listening.

We made a rhythum and went round in circles
Playing it Paul/drum Edd/claves + me/other drum

Assessment of the learning objective, to improvise rhythm patterns, can take place in this last plenary. Using a simple checklist system which lists all the children's names, jot down information about each child in the class as they play in the final performance session.

As the children play, listen and observe carefully. Here are some assessment points for this activity. Although intended to be applied for the activity described above they could be adapted for many activities.

- **Are the children holding and playing the instruments appropriately for this activity?**
- **Is the sound they are producing from the instruments clear and pleasing? Could it be improved if they altered how they play the instrument?**
- **Are they playing a different rhythm each time in the 'conversation'? Is one child repeating their pattern, tending to copy the pattern of their partner?**
- **How interesting or complex are the rhythm patterns – do they have varied patterning and intricate detail – or are they rather plain and simple?**
- **How well do the two children play together? Does each child lead on smoothly and in time from the other, or are there gaps or overlaps?**
- **Do they appear to listen well to one another?**
- **Do the children give a sense of performing their conversation to the audience with confidence and a sense of projection?**

Singing

To teach a song, it is a good idea to start with some vocal 'warm-ups' and preparations for singing as described in the early section.

Let the children hear the song as a performance, ideally with you singing it to them, or you singing supported by a performance on CD. Even if you need the CD for support, it is important to sing too. The messages conveyed by your active involvement in singing are more important than the quality of your singing. Be aware that for younger children, many recordings of children's songs romp along at too fast a pace. At a fast tempo, the children will have difficulty learning the song from a recorded version.

Now break down the song into manageable chunks for learning. How you do this will depend on the age and prior singing experience of the children. With younger children it will be useful to speak the words of the song slowly so that they can grasp the language. They will probably begin to join in and pick up the song bit by bit as you sing it repeatedly for them. There is a strong tradition of finger rhyme and action songs with young children. While these are engaging, ensure they don't detract from the song singing. Learning a song represents a difficult enough task for many children - learning the words, picking up the rhythm and melody of the song, and controlling their voices to match their singing to everyone else are challenges enough. If the song has complex actions as well, this will increase the learning challenge. Research has shown that children will focus on learning the actions and words of a song first, leaving the musical elements until later (Welch, 1998). Songs for inexperienced singers need to diminish the difficulties of language and actions so that the children can pay attention to the musical features.

When teaching a longer song to older children, it is a good strategy to break the song down into smaller sections, perhaps even phrase by phrase. Listen carefully to how the children are singing and give feedback. If possible try to withdraw your singing, or the playing of the CD, and challenge the children to sing unsupported. This is a good test to see if the children can sing the song independently.

As they rehearse a song, children need to be given further aims. The children might be asked to work on:

- **posture, breathing and diction;**
- **singing tone;**
- **a difficult portion of the melody;**
- **varying the dynamics – making changes in loud and soft;**
- **the tempo – experimenting with singing the song faster, slower or with changes in tempo.**

Repeating the song over and over again will become dull and unproductive. Involving the children in the process of rehearsing is a valuable way to develop their appraising skills. Have the children record their singing performance on tape. Listen to a play-back of the performance and discuss how it might be improved. It is also important to consult the children on any musical decisions concerning their performance – should we sing all the verses; does it sound better faster, softer; how might we convey the meaning of the words more expressively; how could we choreograph a performance of the song; on what occasion shall we sing it?

RESEARCH SUMMARY

The processes by which children learn to sing have occupied the interest of many researchers. Graham Welch has conducted a number of studies into this topic and reviewed research in the field extensively. From this work he has been able to establish a set of phases through which children move as they learn to sing. Although he would urge caution in interpreting the phases too literally, they provide a useful guide for thinking about the different processes children will move through. Most importantly, Welch defined the 'developing singer' as a child who is progressing through the phases. If a child cannot yet pitch their voice freely and even sings, as some young singers do, almost on a monotone, the child should be considered as slow to progress rather than labelled a non-singer. He emphasised that children need appropriate support in learning to sing – encouragement, the appropriate repertoire, and plenty of opportunities to practise.

Introducing notations

Children might make up their own notations – often called graphic or symbolic notations because they create their own drawing and symbols to represent the music – or they might learn about the kinds of notations which are used in different kinds of music – such as conventional staff notation, guitar chord symbols.

GRAPHIC NOTATION
Graphic notation refers to a range of invented drawn representations of musical sounds, from the quite free:

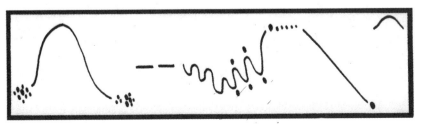

to the more organised and measured:

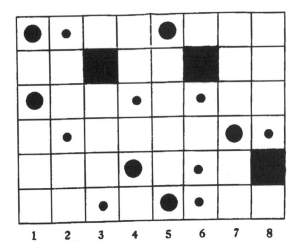

Some contemporary music is written in forms of graphic notation invented by the composers and these can be interesting for children to look at as they listen to the music. In very simple terms, there are two processes to graphic notation – either the children translate musical sounds into visual symbols, or they translate visual symbols into sounds. This translation process – to or from visual symbols – is a valuable learning one. It challenges the children to work out very carefully what is happening in the music in order to convert it into drawn or written symbols – or to imaginatively convert visuals into sound.

Clasroom story

A teacher working with a Year 2 class has prepared a large sheet of black paper on the wall. He has ready-cut large shapes of sticky paper – circles, cubes, lines and zig-zags. Together with the children he discusses arrangements of shapes to be stuck on the paper. As each arrangement is decided upon, the children explore how they might 'sing' the patterns of shapes.

An approach which is very similar to graphic notation, and so I have included it in this section, is to use objects, almost any object within reason will serve, to represent music. Multilink, pebbles, shells, small sticks, straws, ropes - all can be laid out on the floor to capture different dimensions of the music. The advantage of using objects such as Multilink is that they are not final but can be quickly moved and changed, allowing new versions to be quickly worked out.

Classroom story

A teacher of a Year 5 class takes a session with the following objectives:

- *to improvise rhythm patterns using untuned percussion;*
- *to notate their patterns.*

The class is organised into pairs and have one untuned percussion instrument between two. Each pair also has a small number of multilink cubes. They have been asked to make up a small pattern and represent with multilink. They work on their patterns and arrange the cubes. Each pair plays back their pattern and all the children look carefully at the multilink versions. As each one plays the teacher describes the rhythmic patterning.

Then the children are grouped in fours. First each pair teaches their pattern to the other pair. Next the four children work on ways of combining their two patterns. They might put one pattern after another, or see if they will fit together. They might put them together in sequences or as an overlap.

Sometimes children just want to make some kind of record to remember their music from one working occasion to the next. The following notation served this purpose.

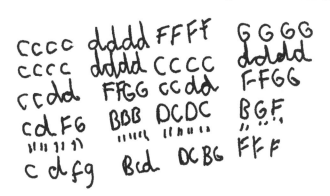

CONVENTIONAL STAFF NOTATION

When children learn to read, they have been surrounded by print and given access to books even before they know what the words mean. In a similar way it is useful to give children access to song books which contain the printed music for the songs they are learning. They are usually very interested to see these. Overhead transparencies of songs can contain the full written version, notation and words. Following the notation of a song melody as they sing it is an interesting process.

It is the combination of pitch notation and rhythm notation that creates the complicated text that is conventional staff notation. Separate out the two and the task of understanding and working with notation is less daunting. There are several explanations and illustrations of rhythm notation in course books and so this next activity focuses on pitch notation, which is less commonly explained.

A CLASSROOM ACTIVITY

Pitch notation is drawn on a set of five lines. The key concept is that notes are placed either between each line or with the lines going through the middle of each note.

Step 1. Provide the children with photocopied slips of paper on which large-scale five lines have been drawn. Invite the children to draw 'blobs' that go up by step (space, line, space, line) or in the same way, down by step.

Here is Emma's melody that moves by step:

Here is Leon's melody, which misses a note each time:

The children can go on to sing or play their patterns of rising and falling pitches. These patterns can start on any note.

Step 2. Explain that if a note on the five lines is to match up with a specific note on an instrument — an F, say, on a xylophone — then there must be a sign at the beginning of the five lines to indicate this. The children might make their own decisions about note-matching and draw their own 'key' at the beginning of the five lines — the staff — to indicate this.

Talking about music

Including in your lesson plan a time when you will talk to the children about the music is valuable in terms of enabling the children to contribute their own ideas and thoughts. Here I have in mind talking about a piece of recorded music, but the same approach will apply to talking about music the children have composed themselves or a song or instrumental piece they have been rehearsing for performance. It is also an important means for assessing children's level of understanding, either as an initial assessment of their learning needs, or as an assessment of how much they have understood and achieved.

Developing a lesson around discussion needs advance planning and is less easy than it might at first seem. In the early days of teaching, time spent scripting out the key questions, key explanations and key instructions for your lesson will pay dividends. Adapting what you say – so that not only the vocabulary but how you construct and sequence your sentences so that they are appropriate for the age group – is an important early skill. It is a teaching skill which many trainee teachers find they must work on.

Imagine the children have been listening to a piece of music played by a group of Chinese folk musicians. The children are gathered around you on the carpet to listen first. They have listened three times now to the piece and you want to focus their attention on the music itself. How do you initiate and guide such a discussion so that the children learn from it?

STARTING WITH OPEN QUESTIONS

The advantage of starting with open questions in contrast to closed questions is that you are allowing the children to let you know what they heard and how they heard the music. First questions might be:

- **what happened in the music?**
- **what did you hear?**
- **can you describe to me some of the things you heard in the music?**

Having asked the open questions, listen carefully to what the children say. A good strategy is to use the counselling technique of repeating back to each child what they said, almost verbatim. As well as disciplining you, the teacher, to listen carefully, it is very affirming for the child to hear their ideas repeated back to them. If you don't understand something the child says, or want them to extend their comments - then ask for this.

You will have a specific learning objective in mind and wish to focus the questioning to develop the children's understanding. It is useful to make a clear distinction between the features of the music itself, the sounds:

- **the speed – how fast or slow;**
- **rhythm – long or short durations, rhythm patterns;**
- **the dynamics – how loud or soft;**
- **the timbre – the actual tone quality of the instruments or voices;**
- **the pitch and melody – whether it ascends or descends in pitch, flows smoothly or jumps;**
- **the structure – longer phrases and then sections of the music;**
- **the texture – is there just one sound, one layer in the music or many layers;**

and information about the music, the context:

- **its place and time of origin – trying to be as specific as possible;**
- **its style – folk song, operatic aria, lament, religious chant etc;**
- **the people who played the music and something more about their culture;**
- **how they used the music – for work, festivals, entertainment.**

Music listening lessons which you might have experienced in your own schooling often focused on information about the music; details of the composer, the instruments which played the music and where and when it was written. While this is useful additional information, the heart of learning in music is to come to know and understand the music itself. Try to lead the children to talk about the music, how it has been constructed and to develop imaginative ideas about the mood, the atmosphere of the music and their impressions of it. However, imaginative responses to music are highly individual and while *you* may hear the music as calming and gentle, the children may have quite different interpretations. Working in arts subjects it is often impossible to pin the children down to 'one right answer'; the imagination is highly personal. This is one of the difficulties of assessing in the arts.

In the early stages of learning to teach, carefully prepare any explanations of descriptions of the music which you will give to the children. Modelling how we talk about music using appropriate terms is important to help children learn how to do this.

Classroom story

Here is a transcript from a lesson given by a PGCE trainee teacher working with a class of Year 3 children. The children have been listening to a recording of a jazz violin piece. This is part of a unit of work in which the children are listening to various pieces of violin music and comparing styles.

Child 1: It was very fast and jolly, it kind of, you know, bounced along, sort of jerky to make you want to dance.

Teacher: It was fast and jolly, bouncy and jerky. What did you think Ben?

Child 2: I didn't like it so much when the violin played all ... all screechy ...

Teacher: You didn't like the high sound of the violin? It could have been because I had it on a bit loud. Carie, would you like to tell us something about the music?

Child 3 (Carie): I don't know really ... (long pause, the teacher waits and looks encouragingly at her). I don't like that sort of music much ...

Teacher: OK, some music we like, some we don't like so much. Well so far, Amy talked about the tempo, the speed of the music, saying it was fast and bounced along. The tempo is how fast it is. Then Ben said he didn't like the sound of the violin playing high, the sound was all screechy he said – what we call the timbre, is all thin and screechy. I don't think violins always sound like that when they are played high up, do you remember when we listened to a violin concerto last week, it was a different sort of sound. In different kinds of music people play the violin in different kinds of ways.

Two children at once, looking at each other: Yeah... it was all swoopy...waah, waah *(other child imitates the sound of the violin vocally)* and on the video we watched she was playing like, like, all fast *(both children energetically imitate the bowing of the violin).*

Several children begin to make vocal and physical impressions of the violinist from last week's music video and the trainee teacher wisely makes a 'damping down' gesture and moves the discussion on.

Notice how the trainee teacher starts with an open question and the children come up with their own ideas. Once the discussion drifts a little, she assembles and reiterates the points, extending them with references to musical terminology – tempo, timbre – immediately giving brief explanations. The terminology is, importantly, linked to what the children have just said and linked very closely to their immediate listening experience.

The children are then asked to compare this piece with another they have already listened to several times and come to know. This focuses the session on the trainee teacher's overall learning intention for the unit of work. This is for the children to learn about different styles of violin music. The children do remember one of their earlier pieces, wanting to imitate the violin playing with a vivid acting out of how it sounded. That the children need to describe the music in their own way, with physical and vocal actions, is very informative. For assessment purposes, it tells the teacher that the children have remembered the characteristics of the music very well but are not yet able to convert this into verbal descriptions. They will need more input from her and more practice at talking about music.

Differentiating and management is built skilfully into this one short episode. Carie has difficulty expressing her ideas verbally and so the teacher invited her directly to contribute. When the children get a bit carried away with vocal and physical imitations of violin playing, a quick decision has to be made as to whether this is a harmless moment of fun or going too far. This is typical of the 'on the hoof' decisions about behaviour management which teachers constantly make. She opts to check their behaviour with a small restraining gesture. Effective management of behaviour is achieved through many minor adjustments of this kind.

Incorporating ICT

Today's children are surrounded by music produced by technology – much more so than live music. At home children have keyboards, access to computer software, internet resources for music, CD and video collections and often unlimited access to music on TV and radio. The gap seems to be widening between children's out-of-school musical experiences – often high tech – and their in-school musical experiences – often very 'low tech'. There is an increasing problem with children becoming uninterested in music as a school subject by the end of Key Stage 2, in contrast to their rising interest in music out of school. Giving children more opportunity to engage in musical activities that are relevant to them and in which they can make a personal and creative input is important. This is a challenge for new teachers.

It is a challenge that holds many advantages. If personal musical skills are not your strength, music technology can provide the musical skills. You, the teacher, need to know the software or equipment well and to be skilful in the teaching skills associated with using technology. Another advantage is that technology enables more individual creative work than is usually possible with conventional, acoustic instruments. And finally, music technology brings the sounds and processes of contemporary music into school music.

However technology cannot replace good teaching. The important question that underpins its use is whether it offers a valuable gain to the quality of children's learning.

At every level, music technology can include the use of CD, cassette and video players for playing and recording performances of music. Children of all ages can record their own compositions and performances, managing the equipment and the process themselves. Using microphones and good quality recording equipment will improve pick-up. Video cameras can be used to record music, dance and drama activities. Simple multi-track recording equipment is available which children at Key Stage 2 can operate.

Recorded versions of songs can be a useful aid to teaching and several are now available with a karaoke version in which the backing only will sound while the children sing over. The full karaoke kit with microphone is an excellent prop to encourage individual performances of songs from children.

Software designed specifically for the teaching of music is plentiful. I intend here to describe the types of learning activities which software can support rather than give specific examples, as these rapidly change and develop.

SKILL PRACTICE
Skill learning, learning to listen and to identify musical sounds, and motor skills to play instruments and perform rhythm patterns can be supported by software which provides practice activities. They are intended for children to work at independently. Typically a small challenge is set on the screen, often with appealing animations, and the child must respond correctly. A correct response produces the next challenge, an incorrect response sets up an alternative route which revisits the same ground.

Some software offers more flexible skill practice in which choices are built in. The children can choose from options or build in elements of their own practice tasks. Teachers also can design tasks that are tailor made for the children's learning needs.

GUIDED INSTRUCTION
This software provides step-by-step teaching of a specific area of knowledge. Notation is the usual area covered by these kinds of software. They would provide a useful means for introducing conventional staff notation, as visual and sound information can be linked.

I intend here to describe the types of learning acitivities that software can support rather than give specific examples, as these change and develop rapidly. (This section is based on categories described by Webster, 2002.)

GAMES

Some software is designed as games in order to increase the children's motivation. Usually the game involves the children in using musical skills and knowledge, or in composing short melodies in order to solve a puzzle or progress to higher levels of the game.

INVESTIGATIVE

Various 'hypermedia' softwares contain musical information and children use them to investigate and explore various topics. Microsoft Musical Instruments is widely known. Illustrations and sound combine with written text.

COMPOSING

This category of software is designed to enable children to compose their own music. The advantage of composing with software is that the difficulties of actually producing the sounds you imagine are removed. Far greater possibilities are suddenly opened up. Musical sounds can be manipulated and transformed using simple commands to vary tempo, pitch, dynamics and timbre. They can be layered to create thicker textures or cut and pasted to produce longer structures. The disadvantages can include the time it takes to input musical ideas into the system and the need to understand the workings of what can be quite complex software. Some softwares get around these difficulties by providing 'ready-made' musical ideas which the child can select and organise.

NOTATION

The visuals of many softwares include symbolic versions of the sounds heard which support children's learning of notation systems. Other softwares introduce notation as a component of their skill learning. Yet others, primarily Junior Sibelius, would enable Key Stage 2 children to write and print out their own music. This software is probably more valuable for the teacher who wants to produce printed versions of music for children to perform from.

Finally, technologies offer fantastic opportunities for mixed media creative work using sound and visuals, perhaps adding to children's performances or culminating in film and animation.

Working with professional musicians

There are many professional musicians who can offer to lead single workshops or longer projects in primary schools. Some are attached to local music services or work as out-reach programmes from orchestras or opera companies. They provide input in terms of specialist skills, often in specific styles of music. One nursery school in Birmingham organised morning workshops from an Irish folk musician, an Indian tabla player, a DJ with a wide range of pop records and a kit drummer. While many of these professional musicians working in education are trained as workshop leaders, some are not. Teachers planning to employ visiting musicians should ask for information of prior experience and references. The workshop or project should be planned as a collaborative enterprise between musicians and teachers. Advance negotiation of roles and responsibilities, making sure expectations on both sides are clear, carrying out any preparatory work as requested are all key aspects of the management of placements.

The great advantage of visiting professionals is that they bring expertise from one key area of music, they bring a fresh approach and they can also provide a means for professional development for teachers (Peggie, 1997). Some directories for musicians in education are available from regional arts organisations.

Management of musical activities

There is an obvious feature of musical activity that makes it trickier for the teacher to manage than other arts subjects – the children are working in sound. Whereas 30 children can all be engaged in individualised artwork in one classroom, a comparative activity for music would be impractical. The possible exception would be a set-up using keyboards and headphones, but I doubt schools are equipped with so many keyboards. Clearly whole class activities, such as singing together or listening to recorded music avoid the issue, but a curriculum that is only built around collective activities will not offer breadth or balance.

The practical difficulties caused by the 'noise' of children working in music, particularly when composing, can be overcome in various ways.

- **A whole class composition activity in which children have allocated turns, perhaps based on a clearly defined structure. They may need to wait their turn, but the emphasis should also be on listening to the other groups.**
- **Composition or rehearsal activities organised as groups, perhaps working in a large room or in separate spaces to minimise the distraction of collective sound.**
- **Group composition tasks which happen at separate times, perhaps timetabled alongside group activities in another curriculum area or other collective music activities.**
- **Individual activity using music technology equipment where the sound is heard through headphones.**

In Early Years settings where it is usual for a range of free choice activities to be provided for, opportunities for children to make music can be more easily catered for. A range of instruments can be set out on a table, or on a carpet area for children to self-initiate music-making activities. It is important, however, that the arrangement of instruments is planned for and changed week to week. It is better policy to plan for one or two instruments to be set out in specific ways than to leave a large collection accessible in a music area. Here are some suggestions.

- **A xylophone and two soft beaters set out on a carpet area.**
- **A basket of small untuned percussion instruments all made of seed pods, set out on a table.**
- **Lots of small bells strung at different heights from a climbing frame.**
- **Three different sized drums put out on a rug outside during fine weather.**

Whatever the age of the children, adult attention and interest in their music-making is important. Listen carefully to how the children play the instruments and you will discover patterns and ways of organising the sound that may not at first be apparent. In more formal classroom settings, providing for children to compose can be difficult. Fixed timetables allocating time slots for each subject diminish the opportunities for integrated curriculum times when one group may be working on a composition task, and other groups on tasks such as art, D&T, dance and so on. Having only one group at a time working in a subject area assists both resource provision – instruments or printing equipment enough for just one group instead of the whole class – and only one group making music is easier to accommodate.

If composition, or small group practising and rehearsing, is organised as a whole class in one large space, much may depend on acoustics of the room itself. High ceilings, wooden floors and no curtains make for a much more resonant working space than low ceilings, rubber tiled flooring and long, full curtains. Organising each group to work on a rubber gym mat can both ease the noise and help with organisation. Equipment is set out on the mats in advance. Each group moves to and from the mats at key points in the lesson.

STORAGE AND HANDLING

Schools vary as to where and how they choose to store their musical equipment. A central storage system is usual, but all teachers share responsibility for the equipment. If the school has a designated room for music, this is where the music equipment is usually stored. Trolleys for storing musical instruments are commonly used and can be wheeled from room to room. Well-cared-for equipment, attractively and accessibly set out, sends strong messages to the children. Fetching and putting out the equipment for a music session and then replacing it at the end of the session can be time consuming. For this reason, you may prefer to plan for specific equipment to be kept in one place, in the classroom, for the duration of a unit of work.

One of the challenges of managing a class of children engaged in instrumental activity is that the children are highly motivated to play the instruments. It can quickly become worryingly noisy. Setting out the ground-rules from the start is important. Giving careful thought to the practical aspects of your lessons contributes to competent class management. Here are some practical tips for first sessions until the children become used to your expectations and used to working in a co-operative and controlled way with the instruments.

- **Focus first sessions on careful use of the instruments. Model how to handle and play the instruments before inviting the children to try. Combine with careful listening to the sound of the instruments and discussion of the characteristics of the instrument and its sound.**
- **Hand out the instruments to children yourself, or invite the children to fetch individually. Set the instruments out on the floor just a distance away from the children. Combine with careful handling, carrying as quietly as possible and placing without a sound.**
- **Plan to use only a few instruments and ideally plan an activity which has a built-in turn-taking routine to ensure equal sharing between the children. Pass the instruments on in a circle game or ensure several repetitions of the activity.**

- Give precise instructions about replacing instruments on the floor or table when not being played.
- Give clear instructions in advance as to when the instrument playing is to stop; with a signal from you, when the egg timer finishes, when they reach a certain point in the activity etc.

END-NOTE

To conclude with aspects of managing music in school, although practical and necessary, seems to emphasise some of the drawbacks of working in music. Yet, music is, above all else, a very enjoyable and exciting activity from which children and teachers can derive pleasure and satisfaction. It enriches our lives, brings people together and provides a means for feeling and communicating which is intangible. As you grapple with the day-to-day practicalities of getting started in teaching, try to hold on to the magic.

Teaching music in the primary school:

a summary of key points

- *Musical abilities are learned from experiences and are not gifted to a minority of people.*

- *Music has traditionally been taught as a whole class, teacher-led activity centred on communal singing. The teaching of music should enable children's own creative and imaginative work in music.*

- *Music in the curriculum covers a range of different activities; performing using voices, instruments and ICT equipment, composing and improvising music from a range of starting points, listening to a wide range of different kinds of music and building up a knowledge and understanding of music which can be applied in different musical situations.*

- *When the whole range of music activities is included and when children are more actively involved in their learning, the teaching of music relies less on specialist music performance skills and more on general teaching strategies, effective application of curriculum and subject knowledge, and successful management.*

- *Children are motivated to make music and find it an enjoyable part of school life. It is a rewarding subject to teach.*

Further reading

Adams, P. (1998) *Sounds Musical.* Oxford: Oxford University Press. Intended for Key Stage 2, this book is full of practical and very 'musical' activities.

Buchanan, K. and Chadwick, S. (1996) *Music Connections.* London: Cramer Music. This is a very comprehensive and useful book of teaching activities which includes CD recording of music used in the activities.

Glover, J. and Young, S. (1999) *Primary Music: the Later Years*. London: Falmer Press. Covering the 7–11 age phase, this book combines theory with suggestions for practice.

Sebba, J. (1997) *Glock around the Clock*. London: A & C Black. A useful guide to percussion instruments and some useful suggestions for activities.

Umansky, K. (1994) *Three Singing Pigs*. London: A & C Black.

Umansky, K. (1998) *Three Rapping Rats*. London: A & C Black. Two books from the A & C Black list which provide raps and stories with songs, mostly for Key Stage 1 but adaptable for older children.

Young, S. and Glover, J. (1998) *Music in the Early Years*. London: Falmer Press. Covering the 3–8 age phase, this book combines theory with ideas for practice. It deals with each of the main activity areas: singing, movement, using instruments, notation, investigating music and composition.

A & C Black publish a wide range of song books, including many primary school favourites: Banana Spits, Apusskidu, High Low Dolly Pepper, and many more, almost all with CD recordings of the songs included.

6 AUDITING YOUR SUBJECT EXPERTISE

This chapter provides four self-audits for you to assess your professional values, subject knowledge and teaching skills in each subject. The assumption is that the ability to demonstrate the knowledge and skills listed is neither finite nor absolute, but developing, and these audits should be used as a checklist by the beginning teacher to determine the range of expertise required to teach each subject in the primary school.

Self-audit of art, craft and design expertise

Adapted from the TTA documentation for Professional Standards for Qualified Teacher Status

I Professional values

I.I Professional values	Evidence
Able to set open-ended tasks demonstrating high expectations of children's achievement in A, C&D.	
Treat children consistently, and with respect and consideration, giving positive and encouraging feedback whilst work is in progress.	
Demonstrate positive values by creating a climate of mutual support and engagement with A, C&D activity.	
Communicate effectively with parents and carers through visual displays of children's work as well as written information.	
Contribute to the corporate life of the school through displays of work and extra-curricular A, C&D activity.	
Involve support staff in planning and delivery of A, C&D work.	

Able to reflect on teaching, to critically evaluate the effectiveness of teaching strategies to children's learning in A, C&D against appropriate documentation.	
Comments	

2 Knowledge and understanding

2.1 Knowledge of A, C&D	**Evidence**
Demonstrate a knowledge of basic A, C&D concepts of: colour, line, tone, pattern and texture, shape, space, form.	
Demonstrate a knowledge of commonly used art processes such as mark-making, printing, painting, sewing, weaving, modelling, constructing.	
Able to keep a sketchbook and understand its value in terms of collecting, exploring, experimenting, designing and other conceptual A, C&D skills.	
Demonstrate a knowledge of commonly used A, C&D materials such as paint, charcoal, paper, card, clay and fabric.	
Demonstrate a knowledge of key subject specific vocabulary.	
Demonstrate a knowledge of the work of artists, craftspeople and designers, and an awareness of sources of further information.	
Comments	

2.2 Knowledge of the A(C)&D curriculum (the 'C' is in brackets when referring to the school curriculum)	Evidence
Demonstrate a knowledge of the four strands of the NC programme of study for Art (Craft) and Design at one specific key stage.	
Demonstrate an awareness of the four strands of the NC programme of study for A(C)&D at the other primary key stage.	
Demonstrate an awareness of the six areas of learning for the Foundation Stage in relation to A(C)&D education.	
Able to link learning in A(C)&D to other areas of the curriculum, particularly design and technology, English and mathematics.	
Demonstrate an awareness of how A(C)&D education can develop an understanding of citizenship.	
Able to use ICT (computer packages, video, camera, CD-Roms, internet) in A(C)&D teaching both in practical art making and research.	
Demonstrate an awareness of ways in which A(C)&D education can promote social, moral, spiritual and cultural understanding.	
Comments	

3 Teaching

3.1 Planning	Evidence
Able to set challenging targets that encourage independence, progression and individual ownership of the A(C)&D activity.	
Able to plan a sequence of lessons, demonstrating progression and coherence in intended learning outcomes.	

Able to group and organise children appropriately for A(C)&D activities.	
Able to prepare effective learning resources taking into account children's language and cultural backgrounds and developing the use of key subject vocabulary.	
Able to share planning with other adults and deploy them appropriately, using their skills to best effect.	
Able to plan for learning in a context other than the classroom such as a gallery, museum or local community.	
Comments	

3.2 Monitoring and assessment	Evidence
Able to use a range of assessment strategies to provide evidence of children's progress towards planned learning objectives.	
Able to give immediate constructive feedback to support children's learning in A(C)&D.	
Able to support children, of all abilities, developing resources matched to individuals' particular needs and interests in A(C)&D.	
Able to record children's achievements in A(C)&D systematically to provide evidence of progress over time, and able to use the information to inform planning.	
Able to communicate such information to parents.	
Comments	

3.3 Class management	Evidence
Able to establish a positive learning environment where children are able to work with confidence and know that their work in A(C)&D is valued.	
Able to plan activities with a clear structure, which interest and motivate the children and reference A, C&D outside the school environment.	
Demonstrate an ability to manage time effectively, particularly in relation to managing resources, and clearing away at the end of lessons.	
Able to organise the teaching space appropriately for A(C)&D activity, with particular regard to storage of materials and health and safety.	
Able to establish good working habits in A(C)&D, and have high expectations of child behaviour to promote self-control and independence.	
Able to work collaboratively as part of a team on such things as displays and school productions.	
Comments	

Self-audit of design and technology expertise

Adapted from the TTA documentation for Professional Standards for Qualified Teacher Status. Derived from those as laid down by DATA Research Paper Number 7 (Guidance for Primary Phase Initial Teacher Training and Continuing Professional Development in Design and Technology – Competences for Newly Qualified and Practising Teachers - with their kind permission) with a few amendments for compliance with TTA 2002.

I Professional values

1.1 Professional values	Evidence
Show awareness of how children develop their ability to design and the various factors that affect the process, including creating a positive working environment for all.	

Recognise that there will be individual differences in the development of their children's ability to design and make and respond appropriately.	
Set appropriate and demanding expectations that demonstrate an understanding of what represents quality in their children's designing and making.	
Determine the most appropriate learning goals for developing children's ability to design and make (including developing and evaluating appropriate teaching strategies).	
Monitor and assess children's attainment in their learning goals (including effective communication with parents and carers of the outcomes and possible ways forward).	
Use the most appropriate groupings for particular learning purposes within design and technology activities that will include working independently and in teams.	
Contribute to the corporate life of the school through displays of work and extra-curricular D&T activities.	
Ensure continuity and progression by planning (with the involvement of others such as previous teacher and assistant) for the development of their children's ability to design and make.	
Comments	

2 Knowledge and understanding

2.1 Knowledge of D&T	**Evidence**
2.1.1 Designing	
Employ an appropriate method through which ideas can be generated, which takes into account the uses and purpose of the design activity.	
Identify criteria for their design proposals.	

Use different methods including drawing (graphic) ICT and other modelling techniques to communicate and develop their ideas.	
Consider the properties of materials when making decisions to meet design requirements.	
Consider different values including aesthetic, economic, environmental, moral, social and technical to inform their designing.	
Develop a plan to make their design proposals that includes strategies to overcome possible problems.	
Evaluate their designs and those of others critically, considering the users and the purpose for which the product is intended and indicate ways of improving their final ideas.	
Demonstrate an awareness of industrial methods and approaches to designing.	
Use appropriate technical vocabulary when talking about designing.	
Comments	

2.1.2 Making	Evidence
Use a working knowledge of a range of materials, tools and techniques appropriate for the delivery of the Programmes of Study at Key Stages 1 and 2.	
Measure, mark out, cut and shape at least one example of each type of material (stiff and flexible sheet, food, textiles, reclaimed materials, materials for frameworks, mouldable materials).	
Assemble, join and combine using these materials and appropriate components and ingredients to produce a quality product.	

	Evidence
Apply appropriate finishing techniques.	
Plan how to use materials, equipment and processes showing how to use alternative methods of making if necessary.	
Evaluate their products critically, showing an awareness of the different strategies they could use in order to identify the strengths and weaknesses of the product they make.	
Demonstrate an awareness of how their outcomes might be modified and improved.	
Demonstrate an awareness of industrial methods and approaches to making.	
Use appropriate technical vocabulary when talking about making.	
Apply appropriate health and safety measures to make risk assessments for themselves and others when using tools and materials.	
Comments	

2.1.3 Materials and components	**Evidence**
Make safe and appropriate use of a range of tools relating to specific materials, components and ingredients.	
Use a working knowledge of techniques and tools for cutting, joining, forming and finishing materials.	
Consider the working characteristics of materials when making decisions to meet design requirements.	

Use appropriate vocabulary for describing materials, tools and processes.	
Make use of ICT to seek information about materials.	
Demonstrate a working knowledge of the techniques of cutting, joining, forming and finishing products constructed with flexible and mouldable materials (including: papers, card, reclaimed materials, e.g. cereal boxes, doughs and clay).	
Mark out, cut and paste, form and deform, efficiently to achieve appropriate fit and finish using suitable hand tools when constructing with resistant materials.	
Using basic methods join and fabricate resistant materials.	
Consider physical and working properties when selecting resistant materials for use.	
Use sensory analysis when designing with food.	
Use effective planning and organisation procedures for preparation, cooking and presentation of food.	
Make effective use of a range of basic preparation skills, techniques and processes with food work.	
Use knowledge of cultural, economic and social influences when making choices with food.	
Use ICT to record design decisions, produce details of planning procedures and specifications to be used with food work.	
Use and make simple flat paper patterns with textile work.	

Use a range of construction and finishing techniques in textile work.	
Use the properties of textiles effectively.	
Apply simple fastenings in textile work.	
Use IT to explore and create shape, pattern and colourways in textile work.	
Comments	

2.1.4 Systems and control	Evidence
Use their knowledge of a range of components when designing and making products, e.g. gears, cranks, pulleys, levers.	
Demonstrate that mechanical systems control energy transfer.	
Describe how mechanical control makes things move in different directions and changes speeds and forces within the systems controlled.	
Use construction kits to demonstrate an understanding of the different forms of mechanical movement, including using linkages, levers, cams, pulleys, gears and cranks to produce linear rotary oscillating and reciprocating motion.	
Describe the movement of one component in relation to another.	
Make use of different sources of energy including electrical, gravity and wind when powering systems.	

Demonstrate through the use of different construction kits an understanding of the advantages and disadvantages of choosing and using different types of drive systems such as rope, chain and belts.	
Use simple pneumatic and hydraulic systems to control movement.	
Use appropriate technical terminology relating to mechanical components and their control effects.	
Explain the basic principles of electrical circuits.	
Use components to construct simple circuits in products taking into account voltage and using fault-finding procedures.	
Represent electrical circuits as diagrams.	
Use appropriate technical terminology relating to electrical components and their control effects.	
State some of the relationships between natural and artificial structures and the environment.	
Describe the ways that structures bear loads, can collapse and become distorted.	
Explain how structures can be stable or unstable according to their design and purpose.	
Identify the importance of structural configuration when using materials and construction kits, e.g. ribbing, triangulation, gussets.	
Use appropriate technical terminology relating to structure.	
Comments	

2.1.5 Products applications and quality	Evidence
Distinguish between aesthetic and functional influences in products.	
Employ a variety of techniques such as investigation, disassembly, evaluation and analysis to appraise existing and predicted products.	
Demonstrate a personal appreciation of the values implicit in technological solutions and consider the impact their own value systems have on children.	
Give examples of quality products and applications in terms of meeting a clear need and fitness for purpose.	
Analyse information gained from appraising products and explain how it can be used to illuminate issues within the designing and making process.	
Use appropriate vocabulary to describe products and applications.	
Comments	

2.2 Knowledge of the D&T curriculum	Evidence
Demonstrate knowledge and understanding of the National Curriculum attainment targets and Programmes of Study in design and technology.	
Design effectively, employing design methods, using drawing (graphic) and other modelling techniques including ICT to communicate their design proposals.	
Make products effectively, selecting appropriate tools and equipment to shape, form and combine materials and evaluate their products as they develop.	

Demonstrate technical language and understanding of materials, ingredients and components, control systems, structures, products and applications.	
Demonstrate an ability to consider different values when designing.	
Apply appropriate health and safety measures to make risk assessments for themselves and others.	
Plan effectively activities that reflect National Curriculum Programmes of Study for design and technology.	
Use appropriate teaching strategies that support children's design and making activities.	
Teach design and technology with confidence and manage children's design and making competently and safely.	
Comments	

3 Teaching

3.1 Planning	Evidence
Reflect upon and demonstrate an understanding of the nature and purpose of design and technology and how it relates to the primary curriculum as a whole.	
Apply skills, knowledge and understanding, where appropriate, from the Programmes of Study of other subjects particularly art, mathematics and science.	
Ensure continuity and progression within the design and technology work with the class to and from which their children transfer.	
Exploit, in their teaching of design and technology, opportunities to develop children's language including technological vocabulary, reading, numeracy and information technology skills.	
Comments	

3.2 Monitoring and assessment	Evidence
Use National Curriculum attainment targets and level descriptions to judge children's performance and to use such judgements to inform their teaching.	
Systematically record children's achievements in design and technology.	
Provide formative feedback to children on their progress in design and technology.	
Prepare and present reports on children's progress in design and technology to parents.	
Comments	

3.3 Class management	Evidence
Maintain a safe working environment, and develop in their children an understanding of the safe use of tools, equipment, materials and techniques through appropriate health and safety procedures and children's routines.	
Create and maintain a stimulating, purposeful, orderly and supportive environment for design and technology activities.	
Use a range of teaching techniques which develop their children's conceptual understanding and their ability to make value judgements in their designing and making which include: • effective planning and time management skills; • demonstration; • questioning; • instructing; • explaining; • feedback.	
Manage effectively and economically their own time in organising and maintaining resources for design and make activities.	
Present design and technology activities and subject knowledge in a clear and stimulating manner.	

Plan and implement design and technology activities that maintain children's interest and motivation taking into account in their planning issues of gender and culture including for example: • avoiding gender stereotypical images, language or actions; • challenging these where appropriate; • engaging their children in studying the distinctive design and technological characteristics of their own and other cultures.	
Cater for children with special educational needs (gifted as well as those with learning difficulties) in their planning and implementation of design and technology activities including providing additional aids and support to assist or extend children's ability to design and make.	
Make constructive use of information communications technology and other resources for learning such as: • story books to generate design contexts; • CD-ROMs; • natural and manufactured objects; • out-of-school visits; • children's personal interests and prior experience; • visits from non-government officers and members of the local economic and industrial community.	
Assess risks related to their own and children's health and safety when planning for and undertaking design and technology.	
Apply knowledge and understanding of safety measures in their own and children's working environments.	
Comments	

Self-audit of physical education expertise

Adapted from the TTA documentation for Professional Standards for Qualified Teacher Status

I Professional values

1.1 Professional values	Evidence
Show awareness of how children develop their ability to become more confident and competent in their movement and the various factors that affect the process.	
Recognise that there will be individual differences in the development of their children's ability to perform competently in different areas of physical education and respond appropriately.	

Set appropriate and demanding expectations that demonstrate an understanding of what represents quality in their children's physical education.	
Determine the most appropriate learning goals for developing children's ability to acquire knowledge, skills and understanding in physical education.	
Monitor and assess children's attainment in their learning goals.	
Use the most appropriate groupings for particular learning purposes within physical education activities that will include working independently, in pairs, groups and teams.	
Ensure continuity and progression in planning for the development of their children's ability to perform increasingly competently in a variety of physical education contexts.	
Comments	

2 Knowledge and understanding

2.1 Knowledge of PE	**Evidence**
Be sufficiently secure in the subject knowledge base to enable the teaching of physical education to be effective.	
Demonstrate and use, where appropriate, technical language that describes actions, movements and skills and correct terminology when describing equipment and resources in the field of physical education.	
Apply appropriate health and safety measures to make risk assessments for themselves and others.	
Teach physical education with confidence and manage children's learning competently and safely.	
Comments	

2.2 Knowledge of the PE curriculum	Evidence
Demonstrate knowledge and understanding of the National Curriculum attainment targets and Programmes of Study in physical education.	
Plan effectively, employing a process of learning in physical education that enables children to learn through planning their work, through their performance and evaluation of their work.	
Provide effective learning opportunities for children by employing appropriate resources (including environments) that promote specific skills and understanding in physical education.	
Demonstrate an ability to consider different children's abilities, the prior and related learning accrued elsewhere, and make provision for all children to benefit from their physical education.	
Plan effectively activities that reflect National Curriculum Programmes of Study for physical education.	
Demonstrate an awareness that PE, like all subjects, makes its own contribution to developing an understanding of citizenship and that all teachers require basic competence in these areas to teach effectively.	
Demonstrate an awareness of ways in which physical education can promote social, moral, spiritual and cultural understanding.	
Use appropriate teaching strategies that support children's learning in physical education.	
Comments	

3 Teaching

3.1 Planning	Evidence
Reflect upon and demonstrate an understanding of the nature and purpose of physical education and how it relates to the primary curriculum as a whole.	
Apply skills, knowledge and understanding, where appropriate, from the Programmes of Study of other subjects particularly science, geography and music.	

	Evidence
Ensure continuity and progression within the physical education work with the class to and from which their children transfer.	
Exploit, in their teaching of physical education, opportunities to develop children's language including movement vocabulary, reading, numeracy and information technology skills.	
Comments	

3.2 Monitoring and assessment	Evidence
Use National Curriculum attainment targets and level descriptions to judge children's performance and to use such judgements to inform their teaching.	
Systematically record children's achievements in physical education.	
Provide formative feedback to children on their progress in physical education.	
Prepare and present reports on children's progress in physical education.	
Comments	

3.3 Class management	Evidence
Maintain a safe working environment, and develop in their children an understanding of the safe use of equipment and resources and of each other, through appropriate health and safety procedures and children's routines.	
Create and maintain a stimulating, purposeful, orderly and supportive environment for physical education activities.	

Use a range of teaching techniques which develop their children's conceptual understanding and their ability to make value judgements in their physical education which include: • effective planning and time management skills; • demonstration; • questioning; • instructing; • explaining; • feedback.	
Manage effectively and economically their own time in organising and maintaining resources for physical education.	
Present physical education activities and subject knowledge in a clear and stimulating manner.	
Plan and implement physical education activities that maintain children's interest and motivation taking into account in their planning issues of gender and culture including for example: • avoiding gender stereotypical images, language or actions; • challenging these where appropriate; • engaging their children in studying the distinctive physical education characteristics of their own and other cultures.	
Cater for children with special educational needs (gifted as well as those with learning difficulties) in their planning and implementation of physical education activities, including providing additional resources, materials, aids and support to assist or extend children's potential to participate to the best of their ability in physical education.	
Make constructive use of information communications technology and other resources for learning such as: • story books, visual stimuli, sound equipment (including musical percussion and other instruments) to generate movement response; • sports and PE literature, CD-Roms, etc; • natural and manufactured objects to promote movement imagery; • out-of-school visits and residential experiences; • children's personal interests and prior experience; • visits from external parties, e.g. professional sports players and sports development officers, and members of the local community.	
Assess risks related to their own and children's health and safety when planning for and undertaking physical education.	
Apply knowledge and understanding of safety measures in their own and children's working environments.	

Apply appropriate health and safety measures to make risk assessments for themselves and others when using equipment and resources.	
Comments	

Self-audit of music expertise

Adapted from the TTA documentation for Professional Standards for Qualified Teacher Status

1 Professional values

1.1 Professional values	Evidence
Reflect upon and demonstrate an understanding of the nature and purpose of music and how it contributes to the curriculum as a whole and to wider school life.	
Demonstrate knowledge and understanding of the National Curriculum Programmes of Study in music.	
Know which skills, knowledge and understanding from the Programmes of Study in other subjects might be applied in music.	
Comments	

2 Knowledge and understanding

2.1 Knowledge of music	Evidence
Listen with concentration and perception to their own music-making and music made by others which will include: • being able to identify some basic musical sounds and processes from listening; • being able to translate sounds and musical processes into dance, gesture, drawn or written symbols, notations, or into words in order to communicate them; • being able to listen, remember and appraise music.	

Take an active part in musical performances with others which will include: • knowing some basic techniques for producing sounds with voices; • knowing some basic techniques for producing sounds with instruments; • being able to keep in time and in tune with others when performing as one of a group; • being able to listen carefully to their own music-making and the music-making of others in order to make adjustments; • being able to present and communicate the performance to an audience expressively, in keeping with the style of music.	
Compose simple pieces which will include: • selecting appropriate musical materials from what is available; • exploring musical ideas and making choices based on evaluation of the ideas; • knowing some musical processes and structures for developing musical ideas; • imaginative and expressive use of musical ideas which are recognised in terms of the musical composition within which they are being applied; • recording work in progress or the completed music using appropriate means.	
Know a range of recorded music and a repertoire of music for performing which represent some differing: • historical times; • cultures; • musical styles; • musical structures and processes; • purposes, social and musical.	
Demonstrate an understanding of musical materials and processes as required to teach music at Foundation, Key Stage 1 and Key Stage 2, through participation in musical activity.	
Know relevant musical vocabulary and terms and be able to use musical language in describing music and musical processes.	
Demonstrate an awareness of different cultural values towards music and how participation in musical activity might reinforce gender, ethnic, religious, social and cultural stereotyping.	
Comments	

2.2 Knowledge of the music curriculum	Evidence
Show awareness of how children develop musical skills and understanding and some of the factors that affect the process.	
Recognise that there will be individual differences in the development of children's ability and respond appropriately.	
Set appropriate and demanding expectations that demonstrate an understanding of what represents quality in children's musical activity.	
Determine the most appropriate learning objectives for development of children's ability across the range of musical activities.	
Monitor and assess children's learning against learning objectives.	
Select the groupings which are most appropriate for learning objectives within music activities and include individual, whole class and small group working.	
Ensure that children's learning progresses by setting appropriate targets in planning.	
Comments	

3 Teaching

3.1 Planning	Evidence
Plan activities that reflect their own subject knowledge and skills.	
Plan activities that reflect National Curriculum Programmes of Study for music.	
Develop the music learning of children across a range of music activities.	
Plan and implement music activities that hold children's interest and motivate them.	
Plan and implement music activities that avoid reinforcing stereotypes of gender, ethnicity, religion, culture or social status.	
Comments	

3.2 Monitoring and assessment	Evidence
Provide formative feedback to children on their achievement and progress in music.	
Involve children in evaluating their work and in setting targets.	
Systematically record children's achievements in music.	
Use National Curriculum level descriptions to evaluate children's musical activity.	
Use all forms of evaluation to inform their teaching.	
Prepare and present summative accounts of children's progress for parents, other teachers or outside bodies.	
Comments	

3.3 Class management	Evidence
Select from the full range of available resources and musical equipment to support children's music learning, including: • information communication technology; • out-of-school visits; • visiting artists; • children's own interests, prior experience and those of their family and community.	
Create and maintain stimulating and orderly conditions for music activities.	
Use a range of teaching techniques which develop children's understanding and their ability to appraise their music-making which include: • effective time management; • modelling; • questioning; • instructing; • explaining; • feedback.	
Cater for children with special educational needs and include additional aids and supports to extend children's learning.	
Comments	

APPENDICES

Appendix A

A sample unit of work for Key Stage I games

A UNIT OF WORK FOR KEY STAGE 1 GAMES

YEAR: One	KEY STAGE: One	TIME (no of lessons):	6 sessions (35 mins approx)	TITLE OF UNIT:	Travelling, sending and receiving skills
				LEARNING OUTCOME:	To extend and develop skills for Games
		CROSS CURRICULAR ELEMENTS:		English - Vocabulary/Language	Maths - Shape/Size/Direction

	LESSON 1 Travelling/Sending	LESSON 2 Rolling/Pushing	LESSON 3 Throwing/Catching	LESSON 4 Hitting/Striking	LESSON 5 Simple Games	LESSON 6 Stations Session
LESSON STRUCTURE AND FOCUS						
INTRODUCTION	Run, travel in own space, stop on command. Game of traffic lights. Pick up a bean bag, put on ground, different ways of jumping over it. Demonstrate to others.	Running in a space with bean bag. Place in space, visit as many as you can, until stop command. Travelling at different speeds, slow and fast. Demonstrate to others.	Travelling in different ways. In a space. Traffic lights. Collect a bean bag. How many ways can you pass or move it around your body? Continue by travelling around room as well as moving around the body.	Travelling around room weaving around hoops, not to touch, in different ways. Walk at first, jumping, etc. Travelling around and visit as many hoops as possible. Stop inside one on command (one each)	Travelling around with ball - when stop command given bounce once. How many bounces can you do before I say stop in 15 seconds? How many times can you pass it around your body?	4 groups and 4 stations. One game to weave in and out of 6 hoops balancing bean bag on hand. One game to make a line in the group. How many times can they throw a bean bag to end person of line and roll back.
DEVELOPMENT	Run in between bean bags. Stop on command. Get a quoit. Touch bean bags with this. Go to own bean bag. Jump over, turn and aim quoit at it. Repeat. Put quoit away. Running with bag, stop, change with friend.	Collect a quoit. Stand near and push bean bag along floor towards quoit to try to hit it. Repeat. Change the pushing hand. Change distance from quoit. Pushing at different speeds.	Collect a ball. Try moving around body also. Demonstrations. Using ball throw and catch in air. Do same walking around in a space. Stand still, throw to nearest person. Change to a bean bag.	Collect a bean bag. Using both hands, stand near hoop and try to hit the hoop. Collect and try again. Collect a ball, throw underarm to inside of hoop, move away further to make difficult. Roll ball to hoop.	Travelling around hoops bouncing ball on command. How many hoops can you visit and roll your ball into the middle of? How many hoops can you visit and hit and catch in the middle?	Throw forwards and roll the other way. One game to travel in different ways. Throw a bean bag in a hoop, next person gets it. Repeat. One game to aim and throw three bean bags at quoits then at hoops. Collect. Alternate the groups. Each group demonstrates one station at end of first rotation
CONCLUSION	Balance bean bag on hand, different ways. Travel around in different ways in room.	Travel around the space with the bag. Send bag to quoit, aim, collect. Repeat. Continue to other quoits around room. Travel around pushing and aiming bags. How many can you hit? Discuss.	In pairs, throw bean bags to partner, changing the distance to make it more difficult. Incorporate work from last lesson, rolling, pushing to partner. Discuss.	Demonstrate to others. Travel around with ball in both hands, when get to hoop, hit in centre and catch. Repeat and try other hoops. Discuss.	With a partner, bounce five times and throw to partner who catches and repeats. How many times can you swap the ball before the stop command. Rolling to partner quickly and slowly. Demonstrate and discuss.	

Resources needed:
Bean bags, quoits, size 3/4 balls, hoops, plastic markers, chalk, feet markers

Attainment Targets - level descriptions	Criteria for assessing attainment
To practise and improve their performance	Has accuracy and control improved? Is there a greater range of travelling, sending and receiving skills?

General requirements across all key stages:
Develop skills of running, jumping, use of space, etc. by experimenting individually, using equipment to send away, receive, hit strike, aim at a target, exchange with a partner, group activities of beating your own score. How quickly? How many times? How many different ways?

POS (general) for each key stage:	POS (activity specific):
To be encouraged to practise and perform simple skills. To follow safety requirements, including lifting, carrying and moving equipment.	To experience using a variety of games equipment, where appropriate. To experience practise and develop a variety of ways of sending, rolling and travelling with a ball and other equipment.

Appendix B

A sample unit of work for Key Stage 2 gymnastics

A UNIT OF WORK FOR KEY STAGE 2 GYMNASTICS

YEAR: Four	KEY STAGE: Two	TIME (no of lessons):	6 sessions (45 mins approx)	TITLE OF UNIT	"Balance"
				LEARNING OUTCOME:	To extend range of balances used in gym sequences
					Health Education, Safety, Personal and Social Skills, Problem Solving
	CROSS CURRICULAR ELEMENTS:				

LESSON	LESSON 1	LESSON 2	LESSON 3	LESSON 4	LESSON 5	LESSON 6
Focus on:	Large Body Parts	Small Body Parts	Shape	Moving Into and Out of a Balance	Partners	Performance
INTRODUCTION	Running and stopping to freeze and hold. Run a few steps jump and land, hold balance.	Move about the hall and on a signal, balance using different parts of the body and different ways.	Run around gym and on signal up to tuck jump and long to stretch jump and wide to star.	Move around gym and respond to commands: left-touch floor with left hand, right - touch floor with right hand, jump - show a shape.	Follow a partner around gym and copy exactly what they do. Repeat but change roles. Emphasise 'balance' movements.	Travel using jumping, rolling, moving onto hands and feet varying body shapes.
FLOORWORK	Explore balancing on a variety of different body parts, eg front, back, side, hips. Holding same base experiment changing body shape.	Explore balance on different body parts on the floor. 3, 2, 1 point balances. Experimenting with different support bases over large and small areas.	Explore stretched/tucked balance shapes around different body parts - contracted around a part, e.g. stomach, - extended, - part extended and part contracted.	Revise the different parts of the body for balancing. Try different ways of moving into a balance: standing, roll, jump. Hold a balance and roll out of it. Find different ways of leaving a balance.	Practise one balance so partner can jump over. Practise one balance so partner can go under without contact.	Make up a sequence with a partner to include a balance, jump, roll, movement on hands/feet. Think about start/end of sequence. Perform sequence
APPARATUS		Practise balancing on low level apparatus on large body parts. Choose two balances repeat them try to change body shape.	Practise moving onto apparatus and balancing on a variety of small body parts. Choose a balance on a large body part and a small body part and travel between them.	Find different ways of balancing on different parts of the apparatus, holding a stretched, tucked or wide balance based around different body part.	Travel onto apparatus and balance –travel-balance incorporate mounting and dismounting using different parts of the body.	Get onto apparatus from different starting points and arrive on apparatus at same time. End with exiting at different times. One balances so partner can go over or go under.
FLOORWORK	Make a sequence of three balances making sure that they flow from one to the other. Hold each balance for 3 seconds.	Choose three different balances on different body parts. Practise balancing.	Devise a pattern of three balances showing tucked, stretched and wide shapes moving between each balance.	Perform a roll-balance-roll-balance using two different rolls/balances. Teach your sequence to a partner and try to learn theirs.	Work out a sequence of three balances so that you alternatively balance and get over a partners balance.	Choose, practise and refine a sequence with a partner that you like. Perform sequence.
RELATIONSHIPS	Individual	Individual	Individual	Individuals and Pairs	Pairs	Pairs

Resources needed:
Mats, benches, box, ropes, wall bars, nesting tables, planks.

Attainment Targets - level descriptions
Find solutions/respond imaginatively to challenges
Practise, improve and refine performance
Repeat movements with control and accuracy
Work safely alone and in pairs
Make judgements about performances to improve
Sustain activity

Criteria for assessing attainment
Class working safely - control
Class answering task - listening, responding
Quality produced in response to task
Response to teaching
Ability to work with others
Accuracy of movement
Evidence of good design
Imaginative performance
Ability to do more than one thing at a time
Sustained participation

General requirements across all key stages:
To be physically active, adopt good posture
Develop flexibility/muscular strength
Develop positive attitudes
Ensure safe practice

POS (general) for each key stage:
How to sustain energetic activity over periods of time
Short term effects on exercise on the body

POS (activity specific):
Different means of turning, rolling, jumping, balancing, travelling on hands and how to adapt, practice and refine these
Emphasise changes of shape, speed, direction
Practise, refine, repeat series of actions floor and apparatus.

Aesthetics The study of (good) taste and beauty.

Appreciation Being aware of, understanding, engaging with artwork.

CAD/CAM Computer-aided design (or drawings)/computer-aided manufacture.

Child profile A document that reports and summarises the progress and attainment of a child in your class.

Colour Visual quality of anything relating to pigment and light.

Conceptual skills Thinking skills, such as comparing, planning and evaluating.

Constructivist teaching The child is not simply given knowledge by the teacher but actively constructs their own knowledge through learning by discovery (discovery learning).

Creativity Ability to produce art, craft or design work using both skill and imagination; improvisation and invention which is not rule governed.

Criticism Evaluation of and debate surrounding art, craft and design activity.

Culture Ideas and customs of a particular group, and the artworks that relate to them.

DATA Design and Technology Association (see resources in Chapter 3 for details).

Deep Intense, strong colours.

Design (n) A plan for solving a problem, considering both function and aesthetics; (v) act of planning, problem-solving and evaluating, often through drawing.

Dimension Direction (rather than scale), line is one-dimensional, shape is two-dimensional (2D), form is three-dimensional (3D).

Discovery learning The type of learning that occurs when the teacher acts as an educational facilitator, guiding the child through appropriate learning experiences.

DMA Design and make assignments. This type of activity provides children with the opportunity to combine their designing and making skills with knowledge and understanding to make quality products (DATA, 1997).

Drone A continuous, unchanging pitch which is sounded throughout a piece of music as a background to the melody.

DTP Desk top publishing.

Evaluate To judge the relative value or success of a process or outcome.

Explore Investigate and research visually or aurally.

Faint Having little colour.

Form Three-dimensional properties of an artwork, existing in space, or the overall structure of a piece of music.

Formal concepts (also called **formal elements**). Concepts of colour, line, tone, pattern and texture, shape, space and form.

FPT Focused practical tasks. This type of activity can be used to practise and develop particular skills, techniques and knowledge that children will need in their designing and making (DATA, 1997).

Ground The surface on which a drawing or painting is made.

Hue Particular colour.

IDEA Investigative, disassembly and evaluative activities. This type of activity helps children understand the world around them through handling products. They can be used to develop knowledge and skills and will act as a source of ideas for children's designing and making (DATA, 1997).

Imagination The ability to think in an abstract way and develop new ideas and possibilities.

Intended learning outcomes The knowledge, understanding, skills or values to be learned in an art, craft or design lesson or series of lessons.

Intrinsic motivation Personal, inherent, essential, built-in motivation. Motivation for oneself not for external reward, but for personal pleasure.

Investigate Experiment and research, both conceptually and visually.

Line Narrow mark without breadth, often denoting a boundary or edge.

Mark-making The act of putting a pigment on a ground, of disturbing a surface, often for representational purposes.

Medium (singular), **media** (plural) The material or process with or through which an artwork is made (such as paint, a material, or print, a process).

Mood The felt response generated by an artwork.

Observe Perceive, see clearly and be able to retain the image.

Outcome The end product of an art making process.

Pitch The frequency of a note, whether high or low.

Print The mark left when one surface is pressed against another.

Programmes of Study Set out what pupils should be taught in each subject within the National Curriculum at each key stage.

Pulse The steady beat underpinning a piece of music.

Record To document something seen, usually through drawing.

Reflection (n) image thrown back off a surface; (v) contemplating how a lesson or an artwork has progressed.

Scaffolding This is the structure or bridge that is created by the teacher to cover that gap between the actual development and the potential development of a child's learning in the zone of proximal development.

Scheme of work A planned unit of learning, with a focus or theme.

Sensual Physically experiencing the properties of material (i.e. through the senses).

Shape (n) a two-dimensional enclosed space; (v) to model or make.

Sketchbook A compilation of visual or written information, usually, but not always, as research for making art.

Socio-constructivist Constructing learning through interaction with others through guided discovery learning.

Space Unoccupied area in or around a sculpture. Area around the subject in a 2D artwork.

Star profile A radar chart used in food technology to show preferences when conducting sensory analysis.

Tactile Experienced through touch.

Textile Fabric or cloth (narrow use of the term); any artwork constructed in a fabric-like way (e.g. woven metal).

Texture Raised pattern, or how a surface feels to the touch. In music, the way sounds are combined: either a single instrument or voice, or many sounding together.

Therapeutic Contributing to a person's well-being or healing.

Timbre The actual sound quality of an instrument or voice.

Tone Relative light or darkness, or the quality of sound.

Tuned Can sound a specific pitch or pitches.

Visual environment How a space or context looks, and consequently feels.

Visual equivalency A mark or visual art that represents something seen, felt or known in some other way.

Visual literacy Ability to 'read', understand and handle visual information.

Zone of proximal development (ZPD) This is the gap between what the child can do independently and what might be achieved through the support (scaffolding) of an informed and interested adult.

REFERENCES

Abbott, C. (ed.) (1990) *Be Safe! Some Aspects of Safety in School Science and Technology for Key Stages I and 2*. Hatfield: Association of Science Education Publications.

BAALPE (1999) *Safe Practice in Physical Education*. Dudley: BAALPE.

Bartlex, D. (2000) Preparing D&T for 2005 – moving beyond the rhetoric, *Journal of Design and Technology Education*. 5(1), pp.5-15.

Benson, C. (1997a) *Design and Technology KSI*. Leamington Spa: Scholastic.

Benson, C. (ed.) (1997b) *First International Primary Design and Technology Conference Proceedings*. Birmingham: Centre for Research in Primary Technology.

Benson, C. (ed.) (1999) *Second International Primary Design and Technology Conference Proceedings*. Birmingham: Centre for Research in Primary Technology.

Benson, C. (2000) Ensuring successful curriculum development in primary design and technology, in Eggleston, J. (ed.) *Teaching and Learning Design and Technology, a Guide to Recent Research*. London: Continuum.

Benson, C. (ed.) (2001) *Third International Primary Design and Technology Conference Proceedings*. Birmingham: Centre for Research in Primary Technology.

Bentley, D. and Watts, M. (1994) *Primary Science and Technology*. Milton Keynes: Open University Press.

Broughton, S., Ellingham, M., Muddyman, D. and Trillo, R. (eds) (1994) *World Music The Rough Guide*. London: Penguin Books.

Bruner. J. (1960) *The Process of Education*. Cambridge, MA: Harvard University Press.

Bruner, J. (1966b) *Toward a Theory of Instruction*. Cambridge, MA: Harvard University Press.

Bruner, J. (1990) *Acts of Meaning*. Cambridge, MA: Harvard University Press.

Bruner, J. (1996a) *The Culture of Education*. Cambridge, MA: Harvard University Press.

DATA (1995a) Enhancing design and technology through the use of IT. *DATA News* (32). Wellesbourne: Design and Technology Association Publications.

DATA (1995b) *DATA Guidance Materials Key Stages I and 2*. Wellesbourne: Design and Technology Association Publications.

DATA (1996a) IT as a tool to support design and technology making. *DATA News* (I). Wellesbourne: Design and Technology Association Publications.

DATA (1996b) IT as a component to support design and technology making. *DATA News* (I). Wellesbourne: Design and Technology Association Publications.

Eggleston, J. (2000) Learning through making: the Crafts Council Research, in Eggleston, J. (ed.) *Teaching and Learning Design and Technology, a Guide to Recent Research*, pl44. London: Continuum.

Eisner, E. W. (1985) *The Educational Imagination*. New York: Macmillan College Publishing Co.

Gallahue, D.L. (1996) *Developmental Physical Education for Today's Children*. Dubuque, Iowa: Brown & Benchmark.

Hope, G. (2000) Draw one and make it - Developing better strategies for the use of drawing for design in Key Stage I /2, Design and Technology International Millennium Conference 2000.

Hope, G. (2001) Beyond their capability? Drawing, designing and the young child. *Journal of Design and Technology Education*, 5(2) ppl06-114.

Ive, M. (1999) The state of primary design and technology in England, in Benson, C. and Till, W. (eds.) *Proceedings of the Second International Primary Design and Technology Conference: Quality in the Making*. Birmingham: Centre for Research in Primary Technology.

Johnsey, R. (1995) Criteria for success, *Design and Technology Teaching*, 27(2) pp37-39.

Johnsey, R. (1998) *Exploring Primary Design and Technology*. London: Cassell.

Kimbell, R. (1994) Progression in learning and the assessment of children's attainment in technology. *International Journal of Design and Technology*, 4(1) pp65-83.

Kimbell, R. et al (1991) *The Assessment of Performance in Design and Technology*. London: APU/SEAC.

Kimbell, R., Staples, K. and Green, R. (1996) *Understanding Practice in Design and Technology*. Buckingham: Open University Press.

Kyriacou, C. (1991) *Essential Teaching Skills*. Cheltenham: Stanley Thornes.

Leigh, S. (2001) Lighting it up. *The Journal of Design and Technology Education*, 6(3) pp223-231.

McGee, C. (2000). Planning and developing a teaching pack for a unit of work for a primary age group. *The Journal of Design and Technology Education*, 5(2) pp145-152.

NAAIDT (1992) *Make it Safe: Safety Guidance for the Teaching of Design and Technology for Key Stages 1 and 2*. Reading: The National Association of Advisers and Inspectors in Design and Technology Publications.

National Advisory Committee on Creative and Cultural Education (1999) *All Our Futures: Creativity, Culture and Education*. Sudbury: DfEE publications.

OFSTED (2002) *2000-2001 Standards and Quality in Education: The Annual Report of Her Majesty's Chief Inspector of Schools in England*. London: Office for Standards in Education Publications.

Peggie, A. (1997) *Musicians go to School: Partnerships in the Classroom*. London: Arts Board.

Potter, R. (2000) An introduction to children's learning, in *Professional Studies Primary Phase*. Learning Matters: Exeter.

Pritchard, A. (1997) Supporting children's learning in primary design and technology with information technology: some possibilities and some teachers' perceptions. *The Journal of Design and Technology Education*, 1 (2) pp 112–116.

QCA (1998) *Design and Technology: a Scheme of Work for Key Stages 1 and 2*. London: Qualifications and Curriculum Authority Publications.

QCA (2000) *Design and Technology: a Scheme of Work for Key Stages 1 and 2: Update for 2000*. London: Qualifications and Curriculum Authority Publications.

Ridgwell, J. (1994) *Working with Food in Primary Schools*. London: Unilever.

Ritchie, R. (1995) *Primary Design and Technology: a Process for Learning*. London: David Fulton.

Ritchie, R. (2001) *Primary Design and Technology: a Process for Learning*, (2nd edn.) London: David Fulton.

Roden, C. (2001) Expert Tutorial *Design and Technology Association (DATA)*, website: *www.data.org.uk*.

TTA (2002) *Standards for the Award of Qualified Teacher Status and Requirements for the Provision of Initial Teacher Training*. London: Teacher Training Agency.

Tufnell, R. (2000) Assessing design and technology, in Eggleston, J. (ed.) *Teaching and Learning Design and Technology, a Guide to Recent Research*. London: Continuum.

Vygotsky, L. S. (1962) *Thought and Language*. Cambridge, MA: Massachusetts Institute for Technology Press.

Webster, P. (2000) High flying feathers: a study support initiative that uses design and technology as the focus for families to learn together, *The Journal of Design and Technology Education*, 5(2) pp132-144.

Webster, P. (2002) Music technology and the young child, in Bresler, L. and Thompson, C. (2002) (eds) *The Arts in Children's Lives*. London and Boston: Kluwer Academic Publishers.

Welch, G.F. (1986) Early childhood musical development, *Research Studies in Music Education*, II, pp27-41.

Added to a page number 'g' denotes glossary.